Angel Investor School

Copyright © 2021 Agustin Rubini and Esteban Rubini

First edition

No parts of this publication may be reproduced, stored in a retrieval system, or transmitted in any form or by any means, electronic, mechanical, photocopying, recording, or otherwise, without the prior written permission of the copyright owner.

This book is sold subject to the condition that it shall not, by way of trade or otherwise, be lent, resold, hired out, or otherwise circulated without the publisher's prior consent in any form of binding or cover other than that in which it is published and without a similar condition including this condition being imposed on the subsequent purchaser. Under no circumstances may any part of this book be photocopied for resale.

ANGEL
INVESTOR SCHOOL

THE COMPLETE GUIDE TO BECOME
A MODERN ANGEL INVESTOR

AGUSTIN RUBINI AND ESTEBAN RUBINI

This book is dedicated to our parents
Vivian and Daniel
For raising us to believe that anything is possible
Without you this book would not exist

About the Authors

Financial savant, investor, and fintech advocate, **Agustín Rubini** is passionate about the world of finance and the future of financial services. Having developed an extensive career in the most prestigious global banks and consultancies, he now spends much of his time advising startups, speaking at worldwide conferences and writing about the world of fintech. He has a passion for innovation and digital transformation as well as a strong background in digital strategy and driving change. He loves coaching and mentoring leaders of startups and is the author of best-selling books such as Fintech in a Flash and Fintech Founders.

Experienced entrepreneur and sales director across some of the largest Investment Banks in the World, **Esteban Rubini** has developed a truly comprehensive investment career. Ranging from traditional strategies and complex derivatives to VCs and Angel Investing, Esteban excels at identifying good opportunities as well as building and developing strong networks and customer relationships. With a Law Degree and an MBA from London Business School, as well as several certificates from prestigious universities, Esteban has a passion for emerging technologies in fintech, blockchain, prop-tech, and insure-tech.

Acknowledgements

Firstly, we want to take the opportunity to thank the more than thirty ambassadors that help us create Angel Investor School. Without their generous contribution, we wouldn't be able to generate insights as rich as we have developed and reach and train as many new angels as we have.

Secondly, we believe it is also important to thank our loyal followers, who consume our content, put themselves in our trusting hands in order to invest their hard earned money, supporting some of the most exciting startups in the world.

Thirdly, we would like to thank our staff, that work endlessly in the organisation of our programmes and investing summits.

Finally, we would like to acknowledge ourselves. We are forever grateful not only for the good times, but mostly for all the challenges that life has brought to us. Thanks to the universe for all the lessons that we have learnt that have made us more mature people and allowed us to write the book to help others in the world.

Table of Contents

Preface 1

Section One: Angel Fundamentals 3
    Angel investing core elements 4
    Should you become an angel investor? 5
    Pros and cons of angel investing 7
    What do returns look like for angel investors? 9
        Here is an example of how this might look 9
    Business angels make a difference – it's not all about the money 10
    Roles that an angel fills for a company 12
        Coach and adviser 12
        Make Introductions 13
        Fundraising 14
        Legal 14
    What is your angel profile? 15
        What is an angel profile? 15
        How do you determine your angel profile? 16
    Traits of a great angel investor 18
    An example path for an angel 20
    Angel investing for the middle class 21
    How much money to invest 22
    How to overcome the loss of faith (and money) 23
        Investments as an educational experience 23
        Investments as a way to help others 24
        Investment as an experiment 25

Section Two: Angel Networking 27
   How to take your first steps in angel investing 28
   Your Investment Capacity 30
      Your Quantum of Investment 31
      Your investment strategy 32
   Meeting startup founders and other angel investors. 33
   Starting out 34
   Where to meet people. 36
      At startup events 36
      At an accelerator program, incubator, or accelerator ... 38
      At a business school 41
      At conferences/Meetup groups. 42
      LinkedIn 42
   Adding value to startups as an angel investor: 44
      Sales expertise 45
      Strategic Advice 45
      Professional Advice. 45
      Industry Insight. 46
      Introductions 46
   Creating your angel profile 46
      Companies you have invested in. 48
      Investment background 48
      Exits or successful investments. 48
      Relevant professional work experience. 49
      Relevant education 49
      Extracurricular activities. 49
      Startup experience 50
      Investment thesis or sweet spot 50
   How to market yourself as an angel 51
   Online and offline self-marketing 53
      A personal blog. 53
      Social media pages. 54
      Angel directories 54

Startup events....................................55
　　Angel investing clubs.............................55
　What is your angel sweet spot?.......................55
　　Sector/industry/geography.........................56
　　Stage of the company..............................57
　　Stage of financing................................57
　　Investment size...................................58
　　Investment type...................................58
　Online networks......................................59
　Generating deal flow.................................61

Section Three: Startup Basics............................63
　Startup culture......................................64
　Startup lingo..65
　The different startup funding rounds.................67
　　Self-funding or bootstrapping, friends and family..67
　　Pre-seed round....................................68
　　Accelerator / incubator funding...................69
　　Seed round..70
　　Bridge rounds (a.k.a. pre-Series A round).........71
　　Series A..72
　　Series B..72
　　Series C..73
　　Oversubscribed rounds.............................73
　　Going public......................................75
　Investing in startups vs. investing in the public market:....76
　Return multiples available...........................79
　How to establish a valuation at an early stage startup.....80
　Biggest pitfalls: why startups fail..................84
　　Pre-investment: No market need or demand..........85
　　Pre-investment: Not the right team and/or poor
　　execution...86
　　Pre-investment: Product (Un)friendliness..........88

  Pre-investment: Poor product / service / business model. 88
  Pre-investment: Legal issues, challenges, and setbacks 89
  Pre-investment: Passion 90
  Pre-investment: Lack of investor interest down the line 90
  Pre-investment: Sector-specific issues. 91
  Post investment external: Get beaten by competition . . 92
  Post investment external: Product mistimed. 92
  Post investment external: Tough geographic expansion 94
  Post investment internal: Pricing & cost mismanagement. 94
  Post investment internal: Lousy or no-marketing 95
  Post investment internal: Ignoring customer feedback and them altogether 95
  Post investment internal: Inability to pivot / adapt quickly enough 96
  Post investment internal: Lack of Focus. 96
  Post investment internal: Disharmony among founders/team/investors 96
  Post investment internal: Lack of Angel's network 97
  Financial issues: Running out of cash 97
 Respecting Milestones 98

Section Four: Evaluating Startups 101
 Investment criteria 102
  Ideas are just a multiplier of execution 102
 Evaluating pitch decks 104
 Prioritizing pitch decks 106
  Problem and solution 107
  Market and Product Offering 108
  Financials 109
  Team 111
 Meeting the founders 113

    Are the founders passionate about their business? 113
    Can the founder describe how they will make money, and is it ambitious enough? 114
    Can the founder describe the product? 115
    Is the founder transparent?. 117
How to evaluate a winning founder 118
    Great founders have a "product sense". 118
    Great founders have a "market sense" 118
    Great founders have a "people sense". 119
    Great founders have a "plan sense" 119
How to prepare for pitch meetings 120
    Specify the purpose of your meeting with the company: 120
    Prepare the right questions: 121
    Scrutinize the company's financials before the pitch: . . 122
Top questions for founders 122
Top questions to ask yourself about the deal. 125
    Is the team right? 126
    Is there a big market for this idea? 127
    Is this idea original and defensible? 127
    Does the idea solve a problem that people want solved? 128
How to perform due diligence 130
    Selection. 130
    Due diligence 132
    Post-planning 132
Company and Sector Research 134
Non-disclosure agreements 139

Section Five: Closing the deal 141
  Investment process 142
  The Term Sheet – evaluating the deal 144
    Contents of the term sheet 152

Capitalization table 161
Investment structures. 161
    Convertible note. 162
    Common stock 164
    Preferred stock 164
    Debt. 166
Typical investment vehicles. 166
    SAFE 167
    UK Seed Enterprise Investment Scheme (SEIS) and
    Enterprise Investment Scheme (EIS) 169
    UK Seedfast. 170
Getting legal support as an angel investor. 171
The bottom line: if it doesn't feel right, just say no. 173
Keeping notes and memos 174

Section Six: Portfolio Management 177
Asset allocation. 177
Start with a portfolio mindset. 178
The number of investments and amounts per investment. 180
Should your portfolio be invested across different
sectors?. 183
Diversification 185
Developing an investment thesis. 186
    How to create an investment thesis. 187
    Still needing inspiration? 188

Section Seven: Investing as Team - Syndicate, and Others 193
Syndicates 194
Purpose of investing as team 195
    Where and how to find angel investor syndicates 196
Benefits of syndicates to startups. 197
    Larger and more efficient funding. 198
    Capitalization table 198

    Wider resources 198
    Startups can stay focused. 199
How the syndicate process works 199
    Opening phase 200
    Investment deal 200
    Closing the deal 201
    Tracking. 201
    Termination of investment 201
Syndicate structure and cost 202
Special Purpose Vehicle (SPV) 203
Traditional fund 204
Lead investing in syndicates 204
Functions of a syndicate lead 205
Qualities of a lead syndicate 206
Crowdfunding 206
Types of crowdfunding 207
    Donations 208
    Debt 208
    Reward 209
    Equity 210
The challenges of crowdfunding 210
AngelList syndicate system 213
    AngelList SPVs 213
How to invest in early-stage funds 214
    What is your strategy? 215
    Investment thesis 216
    Other considerations 218
Angel groups or clubs 220
Active angel investment groups 222

Section Eight: Life as an Angel Investor 225
Can you be a full-time angel investor? 225
How profitable is angel investing? 227

The day to day of an angel. 227
How often does an angel speak with the founders? 229
Setting expectations 231
Being a strategic investor. 233
Being a mentor 234
Being a coach 235
Becoming part of an advisory board 237
Taking a seat on the board of directors 238
Some top angel investors you should know about. 241
    The way to being a super angel: the story of Fabrice Grinda 243
    Successful angel, successful VC? The story of Ullas Naik 244
    The story of Eneko Knörr and AngelClub.es 245
    Enter the Angels' Den of Bill Morrow. 246
When to quit. 246
Rounding it up. 247

Preface

Here's to the crazy ones, the misfits, the rebels, the troublemakers, the round pegs in the square holes ... the ones who see things differently – they're not fond of rules ... You can quote them, disagree with them, glorify or vilify them, but the only thing you can't do is ignore them because they change things... they push the human race forward, and while some may see them as the crazy ones, we see genius, because the ones who are crazy enough to think that they can change the world, are the ones who do.

It is not clear who wrote the iconic quote above, but this was made popular by no less than Steve Jobs from Apple, who excelled at promoting their Think Different motto. When we read it, we thought it could well apply to angel investors. They hunt for the best entrepreneurs, champion them, and support them financially so that their crazy ideas can crystallize and become realities. While doing this, angel investors are a bit crazy themselves, as being successful in this investment role is not an easy job.

That's why we love angel investing. It offers the chance to help dreamers that are trying to change the world, from all walks of life, from all geographies. This book is going to teach you modern angel investing.

Angel investing has changed a lot with time. As a little sibling of venture capital and as a deep champion of technology, angel investing is being conditioned by changes that are experienced in these fields. Venture capital has become a lot more widespread and popular globally; it is no longer limited to Silicon Valley and a selected few. Technology and information are now making the process of investing slicker by cutting due diligence and finding the right companies for the right angel investors.

Anybody can become an angel investor. You just need to find a company, get inspired by the founder, write a check, and go back to sipping your Martinis. However, not everybody will become a successful angel investor.

In this book, we will cover all the basics about angel investing so that you are ready to decide on whether this path is right for you and how to get started. Notice that we have said angel investor path, as we believe this is a long and steady journey. Like practicing a sport and becoming good at it, angel investing will take time. Time to develop your skills and time to build assets that you can count on to become more successful.

When it comes to skills, there are several technical tools and measures that you need to comprehend. However, you will also need to learn how to read people and how to trust your gut. And your gut will get better as you meet more founders, invest and reject deals, and get involved with the right, and wrong, companies.

In this journey, we are not alone. We have spoken with hundreds of the best angel investors in the world, and these have altruistically shared their knowledge and best tips so that you can benefit from them.

If, after reading this book, you think you want to be an angel, we would be delighted to count you into one of our programs at Angel Investor School.

Agustin and Esteban

SECTION ONE
Angel Fundamentals

In this chapter, we will discuss the basic elements of angel investing. These topics are essential to help you decide if your interest is worth the effort.

Let's start by defining angel investment. Technically, angel investment is a form of venture capital that involves individuals or groups of individuals investing money in a small, early-stage company or business.

There are no "formal" qualifications to be considered an "angel" outside of one's own opinion. Many people define what an "angel" is, and that definition may differ from yours. The bottom line is that anyone can be an angel in this sense.

Let's take a look at some of the core elements of angel investing.

You may be wondering how the angel investing term got coined. It all started on Broadway, in the theater business. Rich individuals were supporting theatrical performances; they paid up startup costs for projects that would otherwise have to shut down and would then get paid their money with interest once shows started to earn revenues.

Angel investing core elements

In angel investing, one or more people invest money in a startup that typically has little or no revenues in exchange for equity or shares in the company. This is generally done as a pre-step before the company goes to venture capital seeking funding. Also, angel investing is usually done after founders used their own funding (also known as bootstrapping) as well as funds from friends and family.

In angel investing, the investor typically provides capital to the business owners or founders in exchange for equity or partial ownership of the company. There is no set amount, and this will vary in different geographies and industries, but the typical investment amount ranges from $25,000 to $250,000.

Angel investors are often individuals that have some experience with small business ownership and entrepreneurship. They typically invest their own money into startups or businesses that they believe could be successful. These investors are sometimes experts in specific industries that can help them identify and provide feedback on a business idea or opportunity's viability. Many angels have devoted their entire life to a specific industry or sector, and their knowledge and networks often prove vital for the success of the startups.

There are many angel investor profiles. It could be an individual with a retired financial background that possesses the time and resources to pursue this kind of investment. It could also be someone who was in the financial sector and now has a pension and other investments that require little attention, so they are looking for additional investments to make with their wealth.

Other individuals may come from an accounting background where they have worked for many years for large corporations or even started their businesses before moving on to a different career.

In short, there are many kinds of angels. They can fall into several categories, but we think a good way to classify them is by the amount they are willing to invest in a business at one time (or their average check size). Below is a list of angel groups by investment size:

- ✓ Enthusiast angel: From few dollars to $10,000 per investment
- ✓ Professional angel: $25,000 – $200,000 per investment
- ✓ Entrepreneurial angel: $200,000 – $500,000 per investment

We shall expand on these categories further into the book in Section Eight when we talk about life as an angel investor.

Should you become an angel investor?

A prerequisite for becoming an angel investor is to have spare cash and enjoy investing in new opportunities that excite you. If you are just doing it for the financial returns, we believe there are better options with much higher degrees of certainty, less volatility, and much more liquidity.

It is also important to have a skillset that will benefit the startups you are investing in, for example, being an expert on either the industry you are investing in or the investment you are making, though this is not always required. Angel investing is highly risky, so don't go investing your retirement savings in startups. If you can't afford to lose the money allocated to these investments, don't become an angel investor.

When an investor in the stock market chooses a company, their primary goal is a return on their investment. The case for angel investors is slightly different. Of course, financial motivation is possibly the highest on the list. However, angel investors know that many of the companies they will invest in may disappear and hence will expect that outcome, something that investors in the stock market view as remote.

Angel investors instead will want the company to grow and become more valuable, which means they can sell their shares for more than they paid for them one day. But the whole journey from zero to hero (not to sound cheesy) is a truly rewarding experience. Becoming involved with their growth, their first contracts, the development of the first prototypes, etc., is what many angels aim for. The financial rewards will follow shortly. Angels also expect the company's management team (CEO, CFO, etc.) to be honest with them and regularly update them on how the company is doing. They expect the founders to be competent when regularly updated while managing their money. They expect them to run their business ethically. Finally, they expect the startup to want them to create something that their customers will appreciate, to solve a big enough problem so that many people will want to pay for it. Some people go beyond that and expect traction coming from a startup. Like one of our ambassadors, Bill Morrow, founder of AngelsDen.com, who doesn't invest in very early-stage startups:

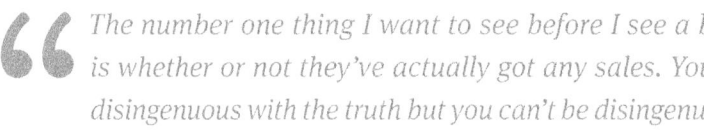

> *The number one thing I want to see before I see a business is whether or not they've actually got any sales. You can be disingenuous with the truth but you can't be disingenuous with money coming into your bank account."*

If the company grows and becomes more valuable, investors may decide to exit that company at a profit. If the company is not performing well, then they may want to sell their shares to other people who want to buy them (if it's a good deal). There is always the possibility of getting nothing in return.

Pros and cons of angel investing

Even though risky as a profession or hobby, angel investing can provide amazing benefits.

Firstly, angel investing allows for asset diversification and is completely uncorrelated with other investments. Generally, startup investing doesn't follow any other asset classes in its pricing and valuation. It is a high-risk, high-reward category.

Secondly, angel investing can provide professional satisfaction, as it can be very intellectually satisfying to follow what a startup is doing and add value to it. Just like solving a puzzle or cracking a code, building something useful and valuable will be rewarding in itself. And learning during the process too.

Thirdly, angel investing provides excellent networking opportunities, allowing you to meet talented founders, investors, partners, and others inside the relevant community. New personal connections will tend to generate other connections and opportunities, both in the personal and business aspects of your life.

Fourthly, it can help you raise your profile and gain board positions or advisory roles in other startups.

Fifthly, angel investing can offer great opportunities to learn about an industry and about the startup world, real-life experiences that an MBA will not provide. You will have direct insight into the newest trends in technology by looking at pitch decks, attending events, and following up on the progress of your investments.

Finally, angel investing can provide mega returns on your investments. Imagine you had invested in a company such as Facebook or Zoom on day one. Even if it had only been $10,000. Your return would have made you a millionaire by the time these companies hit the IPO stage.

Now that you know the good, it is important to know the bad. In short, angel investing is hard and can lead to the complete loss of your investment. When you invest in the stock market, for example, in NASDAQ or FTSE, you usually see the value of companies going up, on average, in the long term. History has demonstrated an upward movement in the stock market, and if you can hold your investment for the long term, you are likely to have a positive return. Companies in the stock markets are usually mature, established, and regulated. Most early-stage companies don't make it this far, and there will be few chances of exiting your investment. In this sense, the option to hold your investment for the long term and wait for the company to recover is just not there, as a failing startup simply disappears.

Moreover, returns for startups are only to be expected in the long term, as the companies need to go through growth stages before being able to pay back. The liquidity is close to non-existent, so if you see that a market is changing, it will be very hard for you to exit. However, you will have the chance to guide the founders in a new direction to sort out changing markets, allowing the company to pivot easier than how a big company would be able to.

Finally, there will be enormous amounts of frustration and disappointment in your journey. These will happen in many ways, but certainly when you can't find good companies to invest in, or when your investments, those you were completely sure were the next unicorns, fail. Until you learn that angel and startup investing is a numbers and probabilities game, you will need to work hard to move past these frustrations and learn from each and every situation, allowing you to become a successful angel. We will talk more about how to overcome this frustration below.

The journey you decide to take is a journey with many unknowns and where judgment ends up being more important than analysis as you have so few data points.

What do returns look like for angel investors?

Angel investors manage to get a return on their investment when they can exit a company by selling all or part of their holdings. This happens at a liquidity event. A liquidity event is an acquisition, merger, initial public offering, or other event that allows founders and early investors in a company to cash out some or all of their ownership shares.

Even though the IPO is the dream finish for an angel, which would mean the startup is likely a unicorn and liquidity increases dramatically, a liquidity event for investors may also happen much earlier than an IPO or trade sale. Very often, angel investors are given a chance to cash out when startups go through funding rounds known as "Series", and institutional investors are keen to clean their capitalization tables. Angels and other investors may have the option (or sometimes the obligation) to exit their investment at the next round of funding. We will discuss cap tables in Section Five.

Here is an example of how this might look

An investor invests $100,000 in a company in its early stages at a valuation of $1 million. This means they are receiving shares worth 10% of the company. The company will then use the cash to fund its business, prototypes, marketing, hires, etc., and attempt to reach certain milestones. As the company grows, it will likely need to raise additional capital at higher valuations. Assuming the company did well, they will raise Series A funding, for example, at a valuation of $20 million.

The investor, in this case, would be the owner of 10% of a $20 million company; that is, they will have shares worth $2 million or 20x their investment.

Depending on the legal documentation and the terms of the new funding round, the angels may choose to exit or keep their shares, which will likely be diluted in the funding round. We will discuss dilution in Section Five. In any case, and despite dilution, the returns should be massive for performing companies and simply zero for those that don't make it, making the math quite straightforward. We have prepared a spreadsheet to help you understand how diversification and successful companies will return very decent IRRs. Be sure to sign up to Angel Investor School for access to plenty of resources.

Business angels make a difference – it's not all about the money

Our ambassador Gokul Rajaram put it really clear:

> *It should never be about the money. I think it should be about one or the other of learning or supporting. If you do those two things, well, the good news is that the finance will absolutely come. But it'll take years. It takes years and so it has to be a long term thing. You have to have a long term perspective on it."*

Startups require a lot of help and guidance to get to the finish line. Most startups fail, but some that succeed can do so spectacularly. Most investors do not know this when they start as angel investors. They are unaware that they will be helping companies grow and that it is more than just about making money. They do not realize how much impact they will have on startups until they become active business angels.

When an investor gets involved in startups, they should expect to help the startup team with any issues that help them push their businesses forward, adding value. This is a big part of the investment process beyond just putting money into the company.

As an investor, you must be prepared to work for your investment returns and help with critical issues that may come up during a startup company's growth stage. If you are not willing to do this, then a full-on angel investing approach may not be the right thing for you at this point in your life. This is why it is essential to understand what it takes to become an angel investor before committing capital into startup business ventures that are ill-suited for you because of your lack of experience in the sector or industry you are attempting to invest into.

Gokul continues:

 I strongly believe that angel investors do not just provide financial capital. I think especially at the early stages, we are seeing a breakup of human capital and financial capital. As some of the earliest backers of the company even before it has product market fit or even before a product in the market, and definitely before the company has an executive team, angel investors need to be close advisors to the CEO of the company.

They need to be the human capital for the company and volunteer their time to help the CEO and company and this is as essential as money. This can take the form of helping the company hire great people, helping the company and strategic decisions as to how to think about the product. How do you think it would go to market and then help the company with customers? How to acquire customers? So all aspects of the company. The CEO and the initial team, they basically need

to be surrounded by great people. Many times, angel investors are successful businesspeople, operators, investors, etc., in other areas that can bring their insights, their network, their talents to help the company. That's as big a source of value that angels can add as financial capital."

Bill Morrow complements this view:

> *So, for me, it's about finding opportunities to mentor at that level. And often the very best investors are the ones that give their advice away for free. They're not investing, they're not involved financially with the business. Those people can find out what it is that they want to do, can find out what it is that they need to learn from the marketplace and how they can give back to the companies that they eventually invest into. So for me, it's about actually helping the local ecosystem, no matter where you are in the world, and finding out what the specific problems are. Finding out whether or not you are actually the person who should be investing, who should be mentoring. Have you got the contacts that you think you have got? It's about the value that you can bring."*

Roles that an angel fills for a company

Coach and adviser

This is one of the most common roles that an angel investor plays. The investment is not just about money; it is also about helping the startup with their business strategy and direction over time. This is a big task for most startups, and they will have no idea how to do this without some guidance from an outside investor. This will be a critical role for any angel investor to fill, regardless of whether you are working with an existing company or a new startup.

The first thing a good angel investor will do is provide some mentoring to help the startup team. This can help them identify issues that may need to be addressed and provide a framework for managing them. Any sort of help may be vital in the early stages, and it can take any form, from testing a product to helping them with customer service issues.

Make Introductions

One of the most significant issues that startups face in their early stages is getting introductions to key players in their industry. The startup may not have a big contact list to use to help them access the right leaders in their field. This is where an angel investor can play a critical role.

As an angel investor, you should provide introductions to key individuals who can help with its growth, success, and funding. This could be investors, potential customers, or other influential individuals who may help with critical issues or provide advice to help the company forward.

It's useful to hear Laurel Touby's view on staying in touch and how this can lead to being invited to a follow-up investment:

A lot of angels will not have an option to follow-up. So it's extremely important that you stay in touch with that founder throughout their journey, good or bad. Every month, you should ping them and ask them: do you need help with anything? Are there intros you'd like me to make? Can I help in some way? Can I roll up my sleeves? I really want to be there for you. And sometimes you should just be thinking about what their needs might be and anticipate them and reach out and say, Hey, I met somebody who I think could be your partner. You know,

here's x, don't do a blind intro, but definitely forward them some information and ask them if they would like an intro and be respectful. Because if you aren't staying in touch, your hottest companies are going to raise without you, they're going to forget all about you, and you're going to be left in the dust. And that's important if you're an angel, because you need to have ownership."

Fundraising

Since angel investors make investments without getting involved with the company's day-to-day operations, they must take on some fundraising roles to assist startups when they run short of cash during their growth stages. Many startups are undercapitalized during their early days and need additional financing to move through their life cycle toward their eventual exit event.

Angel investors will often fill this role for startups in need of capital when they want to move quickly and do not want to wait on external financiers or banks that may not have a lot of experience working directly with startups at this stage in their development.

Legal

Startups rarely have the resources to hire an outside law firm or even an internal legal team to help them through some of the legal issues that will come up as they grow. Angel investors can become a valuable source of legal advice and assistance for startups that they invest in.

You also need to consider how much time you have available to commit to these kinds of activities. If you are running a small business yourself, you may not have the time or bandwidth to invest in a startup company's roles. Ensure that you understand what is expected of you if you decide to become a business angel investor with some of your wealth and disposable cash before investing in startups. This will allow you to make smarter decisions about where and how much capital you want to deploy. You need to be able to do this before investing, as it becomes too late once the funds are deployed and you are involved in an investment situation that requires more work from an angel investor than what is available for you.

What is your angel profile?

Finding your angel profile is a critical first step for aspiring angel investors. It is how you determine the kind of investments that you should make.

You can use your angel profile to:

1. Determine the type of investment opportunities that you are most comfortable with.

2. Learn about the different types of angel investments and which areas you will most likely be drawn toward.

You should keep in mind, as well, that your angel profile may change as you gain experience in angel investing. As with any field of endeavor, the best way to get better is to remain open-minded and flexible so that you can improve over time.

What is an angel profile?

Your angel profile is a set of investment criteria that will help you choose the investments that fit into your current stage of investing. It includes the industry or niche within an industry that you are most comfortable with.

For example, if you have a finance and technology background, you may find that your angel profile fits best with early-stage technology companies. If you have a background in marketing and consumer products, you may find that your angel profile fits best with early-stage consumer product companies.

Each person has their own unique angel profile because we each bring different experiences to this field. Our previous work experience can influence which deals we find most attractive. Our hobbies and personal interests can also play a role in our angel profiles because we tend to be more comfortable with investments that use our skills and knowledge. Finally, our personal and business network will also guide where we source deals and how we may help the deals we choose to get involved with.

Your angel profile will change over time as your knowledge and experience grow and your interests change. Suppose you are just starting out as an angel investor. In that case, it is essential to understand how to identify the different types of opportunities that fit into your current investment profile so that you know how to search for them online or through other means without wasting too much time searching in areas where you will not be successful. You also need to understand the types of deals that are not right for you to avoid bad deals and avoid spending too much time and money.

How do you determine your angel profile?

You can take a simple approach to build your angel profile

1. Review your past work experiences or other life experiences, and

2. Identify the types of companies or investments that interest you most.

To determine your angel profile, answer the following questions:

What areas do you have experience in?

These areas may include a specific industry or business area (such as AI or banking), or they may be more personal interests you have (hobbies like chess or causes like environmental change). Review all of the areas that interest you and note those that stand out as areas where you have had some experience. These are the areas where your angel profile is likely to be most vital.

For example, suppose you have a background in technology. In that case, you may have worked for a cloud computing company or big data business. If you have experience working as an engineer or software developer, this will be an important area of your angel profile. You will understand the challenges that these companies are likely to face and ask the founders' important questions and validate whether they have a grip on the issues. You will know the industries' problems and what the product market fit may look like in a particular company.

How does your angel profile relate to your existing work experience?

Review all of the areas that interest you and note those directly related to your work experience. For example, if you are interested in technology and have a background in financial products, your angel profile may be most robust in fintech investments. If you have the most experience in marketing and sales, you may want to focus on growth marketing and influencer marketing startups.

What types of companies do you find most interesting?

Review all of the business areas that interest you and make a note of those that are most interesting to you. Which markets or issues do you feel passionate about?

You might want to look at the current hot topics in the world, such as 5G, self-driving cars, blockchain, augmented reality, and the likes. Hot business areas such as these, as well as others like life science, alternative energy, and no code software, can give you a chance of achieving a good return on investment because there is high interest in these products and services in the marketplace and your startup may be able to get a share of that market.

Suppose insurtech companies interest you, and you happen to

work in corporate insurance operations. In that case, you may want to focus on corporate insurance companies as your main angel profile. Or imagine that you are especially interested in augmented reality products but have no background in this area; you may still want to invest in this area and make several small investments in order to learn about the industry. As long as you feel passionate about the industry or the problems that a specific sector or tech may solve, then you are on a good path. Without passion and deep involvement in the issues at hand, angel investing becomes just another form of investing, and you may find better return opportunities.

Traits of a great angel investor

The best angel investors can connect the dots between a company's potential and the market, and they can make the right decisions at the right time. Angel investors who are willing to back meetings with startup investments have a better chance of succeeding than those who just want to stay on the sidelines.

Entrepreneurial

The best angel investors are often entrepreneurs themselves. They know how hard it is to start a company, and they have empathy for it. They also have experience of what it feels like to fail, and they can see when others are going in that direction.

You should be able to follow your gut instinct in choosing investments. It pays off if you can predict trends by connecting the dots correctly. You should also do as much research as possible before putting your money into any investment, and you should always learn from your decisions and mistakes.

Ultimately, business founders and entrepreneurs are the ones that know best what it takes to become successful, so you should be able to trust their judgment and follow it.

Sharp Focus

Great investors can pick their winners and focus on the big opportunities. They have a good sense of what is happening in the market and a vision of where it is going. They also tend to be more interested in the long-term potential of an investment than short-term gains, and they are willing to put their money into things that make a difference.

They can spot the trends and opportunities that business founders often do not. They can focus on the big picture, and they can see the potential of an investment even if it is in a niche area.

Tenacity

Persistence and patience are two must-have traits. Investors need to be prepared to take the time to get things right. You should be able to stick with a company during its difficult times rather than writing them off when they are struggling. Many angel investors will invest money into a company when it has already had some initial success, so they understand that it will take time for the business to get off the ground. Great investors are confident enough that they do not fear failure, and they are willing to stick with their investment strategy until they make a return on their investments.

Patience

As startup investing takes a long time, both in finding the right companies and in scaling them, it is clear that a great angel needs to be willing to wait until their portfolio of companies is ready to scale, not giving up in the meantime. They know that if they rush things, they will not get the best results, so they will be willing to wait until they are ready for further investment and expansion.

Trustworthy

Great angel investors are trustworthy, and they will do their best to keep their word. They will also be honest with the companies they invest in, and they will not make any secret plans that could harm the company's future growth. They can also gain other investors and business founders' trust, which is key to building a good reputation as an angel investor.

Thorough

Great investors are thorough, and they will do their best to meet the needs of their companies. They will understand what the business needs and make decisions in the company's best interests. When they make investments in a company, they are willing to put in the time and effort required to make sure it works out well for both parties.

In summary, great angel investors often start as successful entrepreneurs who can see where trends are going before others can. They understand how difficult it is to create their own company, so they have empathy with those who need their help. They are also confident enough that they do not fear failure, making them more willing to invest when others might not be willing. They can think on their feet, and they also have a good sense of what is happening around them. They can spot opportunities where others cannot see them, which helps them connect the dots between a business's needs and its growth potential.

An example path for an angel

If money is not an issue, target a large number of companies so that you can find an outlier. Suppose you invest in 20 companies over two years, looking for companies with traction (developed products and some revenue). You invest small amounts on them and save funds for following up on your investments. Let's say you allocate 10% of your net worth to angel investing, which we will assume its $500,000. You could therefore invest $20,000 in each of 20 companies, leaving you $100,000 to follow on in the best companies.

Let's suppose that you lost all your funds; this would mean a hit of 10% of your net worth, which is not nice but could easily happen if you were fully invested in the stock market whenever there are fluctuations. A 10% loss is something you should be able to live with, especially if you are thinking of investing in a risky asset class such as startups.

A more likely scenario would be that, after a few years, you realize that 10 to 15 companies you invested in have disappeared, got sold (at a loss), or went bankrupt. However, if you were lucky and followed a sound strategy, some of the remaining companies are likely doing well and, therefore, would be able to compensate for the losses from those which failed. A return of 20x or 30x is not unheard of in the startup world, not to mention you should aim for 100x or 1000x as happens with unicorns. Even though it may sound like a dream, it is what angel investing is all about. Finding those gems that will change the world and deliver out of this world returns.

Angel investing for the middle class

If you want to join the cap tables of startups, the easiest and most obvious way is to invest your money and capital in normal funding rounds. However, if you are not in a position to invest generously yet, there are still ways. You could otherwise join as an advisor or as an employee, which could provide you with equity and wouldn't cost you any money, just time.

Having said this, it is not required to be a millionaire to become an angel investor. If we just look at Angel Investment Network, a website that offers hundreds of startup investments, we can see that most companies are happy with investments of around $7000, and some even go as low as $1000 to join in. You can find great opportunities to invest in with as little as $10k or $20k. Also, if you have a family member or friend who wants to be an angel investor, you can partner up and combine your resources and invest together. If you want to be an active angel investor, it's a good idea to start small and get your feet wet by making a few investments (and mistakes). Once you get the hang of things, you can increase your capital investment as you see fit. But there will always be plenty of great investment opportunities for investors who are happy to invest in amounts between $10k and $25k per deal. There are several ways and structures to invest smaller amounts of money until you get more experience. Funds, clubs, networks, syndicates, crowdfunding, etc., can be great ways to start and will be relatively painless while still allowing you to contribute (to a degree and depending on the situation), but where you can feel the angel experience.

But bear in mind that the main issue we find is investing in just one company will be very risky. Diversification is incredibly important when it comes to investing in startups. We will cover this in our portfolio management chapter. For the time being, it is important to know that with more money comes more investment opportunities. If you are playing the long game in angel investing and can only afford to invest (and potentially lose) $10,000, there is nothing stopping you from investing this. Just make sure to use it as a training opportunity and engage with the founders.

How much money to invest

When it comes to angel investing, many small investments may be better than a few big ones. The average size of an investment made by an active angel investor is between $25k and $100k per deal. Most investors don't want to commit $100k or more per deal. So while the average size of a financing round for companies that do raise capital is between $250k and $1M, many investors choose not to invest that much money in a single round, especially at the very early and risky stages. Most investors will invest between $10k and $25k per deal in an early-stage startup and then wait until another round of financing occurs before making another investment into the same company (known as follow-on investments).

How to overcome the loss of faith (and money)

As the saying goes, "If you want to know what someone believes in, look at his checkbook."

Despite this, many angel investors lose faith in their investments. They feel like they're throwing money away, and they become afraid to follow up their investment in further rounds.

The problem? They don't know how to think about their investments.

They believe that how they think about an investment is the same way everyone else thinks about an investment. They think that, because they are investing, they need to calculate the ROI of every investment to determine whether or not it's a good investment.

But that's not the way that angel investing works.

First and foremost, you should not think about your investments purely in terms of money. Money is not all that matters in angel investing. What matters is whether you believe in the company and its founders enough to invest in them. You are playing the long game.

So we believe there are a couple of ways to think about your investments:

Investments as an educational experience

Your investment should be an educational experience that will help you to grow as an investor, as a person, and as a human being. This is especially true for your first angel investments, and this is why we recommend you start small.

If your investments are helping you grow, then that means that you're growing as an investor. That's the real reason why you should invest in early-stage companies. Sure, you may lose some money, but if you're learning from your mistakes and growing as an investor, then your losses are worth it.

Gokul Rajaram agrees:

> *Even for people like myself who have a day job, it helps us become better in our own jobs, because you learn something new by working with all of these founders across industries and you bring something back to your job. Time and again, when I talk to someone who's in building a company that focuses on consumer services, I have always learned something from them that I can bring back to my job with DoorDash."*

In order to learn, think about the main skills that make a good angel. Think about the technical skills, think about the industry-specific knowledge that you want to find out, and think about how you can read people better.

Investments as a way to help others

You can also see your investments as a way to help others. This is not to be mistaken with charity though as they are different things. For example, when you invest in an early-stage company, you are helping that company to grow. And, by growing, they can create jobs for other people (they'll have employees), and they have the potential to create value in their community (they'll be able to employ people within their organization). But your motives for helping them must stem from your interest in the product, the problem, and its solution, and the potential to help build something and maybe receive financial rewards. If you are interested in charitable work or donations, that is absolutely fine, but not to be mixed with angel investing.

That being said, we believe that it is complicated to invest in friends and family, as there will be personal connections that interfere with your investing and due diligence capabilities. In this particular case, we think that it is possible to relate both angel investing and charity. Therefore, if you will be investing in friends and family, you may want to consider this investment as a part of your social capital and treat it as charity (unless you are completely convinced by the startup). This will avoid problems with your loved ones, and if one day the startup surprises you, all the better. We will follow up on this as part of Section Five.

Gokul Rajaram adds to this view:

> *Like I said, one of the key reasons that people start angel investing is because a friend of theirs, someone they think is high calibre, high quality, wants to start a company. Angel investing is a great way to support your community, support your colleagues, support your friends who are going out and starting companies. That's the way that many people start. It's a great feeling. I think by doing that you realise you learn a lot, of course. That's why they always used to call the friends and family round as a first round because it's literally your friends and your family who believe in you, who want to support your dreams."*

Your investment is helping others. That means that your losses are worth it because you're creating value for society by helping these companies grow and achieve their potential. And, by doing so, you may also be helping yourself.

Investment as an experiment

You can pretend that your investment in a startup is an experiment.

Think about it this way. If you were to pick up a rock, would you be able to predict what was under that rock? No, of course not. You might find gold, or you might find nothing at all. All you know is that the potential for something valuable is there. So, when you invest in a startup, think of your investment as an experiment. You never know what will happen; you just need to ensure that the rocks that you pick are the ones that have the most potential to uncover gold.

A good example would be Twitter, which started as a side project for Jack Dorsey, Evan Williams, and Noah Glass. None of them knew where the company would go. They just knew that it had potential, so they continued to invest their time and money in it.

In conclusion, the best way to think about your investments may be in non-monetary terms, even though this might sound counterintuitive. An investment is more than just a transaction. Your investment is an educational experience, it's a way to help others, and it's an experiment. You never know when you're going to find something valuable, but if you follow certain rules, diversify and put hard work into it, the rewards will be fantastic.

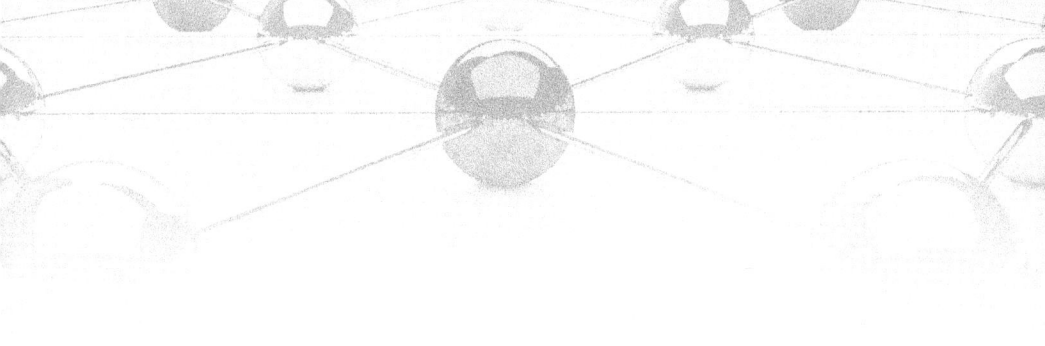

SECTION TWO
Angel Networking

In this chapter, we will discuss how to network with other angel investors and startup founders in order to start and develop your journey as an angel investor and especially to build your name and source the best startups. Networking can be done in different ways.

Let's start by reading how Gokul Rajaram does it:

> *The best way to network is not just hey, let's meet up but the best way is to actually send other angels companies. So when you see a good company, send it to someone else. The reality is if the company is raising a million dollars, you probably will not, as the angel investor, be able to put the whole million dollars. Even if you are, it's probably not a good idea, you probably want two or three people so that the company can benefit from all three of you and your expertise. You can share, help better analyse a company and help the company. And so, I think Angel Investor School and forums like that can be a great way to find other angel investors and network with them. Then finally venture capitalists themselves,*

> as you start investing in companies which are invested in the next stage but with other venture capital firms."

It is important to establish a network of people you can trust and provide support. These people may have more experience than you in angel investing at the beginning and will help you grow and gain experience. In angel investing, knowledge can provide power and leverage. Furthermore, if you can learn from the mistakes of other investors, it will save you a lot of time, heartache, and money.

You can build up your network of angel investors at different paces, though it is a process that typically takes years and never stops. You don't have to call everyone in your network every day or even every week. Just make sure that the people in your network know why you are calling them and what you are looking for. These types of conversations will be more productive if they are not just centered around getting opportunities for investing but also about learning from each other.

How to take your first steps in angel investing

It is good to get a quick helicopter view on how the angel investment process works. This will allow you to better understand the whole process before you engage other angels and founders in your journey. We will dig deeper into all of them throughout the book, so don't worry if you feel that the information in this section is not specific.

In building up a portfolio, the angel typically goes through a cycle similar to the one we will describe below. The first thing you will need is to build your funnel, a flow of companies and startups that will be fundraising. This can be done through a syndicate or your own contacts. The funnel can be extensive or limited, but the idea is that you have enough to compare companies, founders, and pitches in order to be able to distinguish one company from another and make up your mind in which ones are good and which are not.

The next stage is to screen through your deal flow. This means reading pitch decks, meeting with founders, researching the markets you intend to get into, and asking for references of founders and companies. Your goal is to find the needle in a haystack, to find those bits of gold that are hidden and not many can see. Try to find opportunities with a high potential reward and low (relative) risk that fit your investment criteria.

The next bit is performing due diligence on the company, an activity that many find boring but is fundamental to catching the right fish. It is required so that you can fact-check what founders are claiming in their pitch and their financial models. Due diligence can take from 2 hours to 200 hours, so take your time, especially when starting your journey.

Once this has been completed, it is time to agree to the term sheet, which means understanding what you are getting as a part of the deal. Consider factors such as what percentage of the company will you be purchasing? How will your shares be diluted when there are further financing rounds? How can shares be liquidated? What are the investor rights, and how will their shares be protected? How will the founders run the company, and how will they notify the investors? Will there be a board established? Will the angel sit on it? We will dive into term sheets in Section Five.

Next, a legal agreement needs to be created. These documents are longer than the term sheet and cover different scenarios and situations that may arise. They are written by the legal counsel (often paid for by the company, VCs or lead investors) and are not usually negotiable for smaller angels. Finally, the process is completed when legal documents are signed by both parties and funds are transferred.

The process varies a little bit if you are investing as a part of a syndicate, as the fund organiser might need to complete fundraising with certain minimum caps and some allocations to manage, and you will not be required to sign the documents directly with the startup, but instead you will do this through an investment vehicle created specifically for this transaction. It is likely that if you invest through a syndicate, you will not necessarily be in contact with the company directly, but the lead in the syndicate will be the point of reference. We will cover syndicates and other ways of investing in Section Seven.

Once you have decided that angel investing is right for you, you need to decide the quantum of investment you want to utilize in terms of your investment capacity and the amount of investment you are comfortable with. Secondly, you need to find the type of companies you are looking to invest in. You can adapt your goals and amounts as you gain experience. As our die-hard ambassador Brad Feld enlightens us:

> *Originally, my goal was to run a marathon in every state by the time I turned 50, and I'm 54. So I clearly didn't accomplish that goal. But like every good entrepreneur, I've just modified it. And so now my goal is simply to run a marathon in every state before I die."*

We will briefly discuss the main points you need to take into consideration when starting your investment career.

Your Investment Capacity

Your investment capacity is defined as how much money you can invest in angel investing as a whole.

This should include your liquid cash, bank balance, and also your portfolio investments. You can also add any other assets that you have that are intangible to this number. Your capacity should be big enough to accommodate your investment decisions as well as your business decisions. It is important to know your maximum capacity because if you don't, it will be difficult to decide how much you should invest in each company. It will also be good for your mental health, as angel investing should never generate stress in your financial well-being.

Your Investment Capacity should also include your time and effort investment. This includes returning phone calls, attending meetings, performing due diligence, etc.

This is just to illustrate that your investment decisions should be in alignment with your capacity.

Your Quantum of Investment

Your quantum of investment is defined as what amount of money you are comfortable with investing in each startup on average. This can be different for each startup, but many recommend that you allocate a similar (or equal) amount to each investment as many investments will generate random returns, and spending time allocating a different amount to each startup may seem arbitrary.

For example, a good way to start is to allocate a fixed amount or a percentage (say 10%) of your liquid net worth. For the sake of argument and to keep things simple, assuming you have a liquid net worth of $2 million, then allocating 10% of it to angel investing will render $200,000, which you could divide into eight companies at $25,000 each. We will discuss investment strategies below.

The type of companies you will be after will depend on what you are looking for. If you are looking for a startup where you may have significant influence, a good place to start may be to invest in startups that are valued at under $500k because these startups are usually early stage, have high growth potential, and not many people in their cap tables yet, meaning your participation could be higher than in other companies.

After you have invested in a few companies, you can decide if you want to invest in larger companies or not. The advantage of investing in larger companies is that they are more stable, typically having more cash reserves and bigger teams. This means that they can make a bigger impact on the world with their product, service, or cause. However, these companies also have different risks than smaller companies due to a higher burn rate. There are also more competitors at more mature stages, which may lead to other competitors taking market share from them. And, of course, their valuations tend to be higher, so you will get fewer shares for your money.

It is important to pick an amount that is realistic for you. If you invest too little, then your impact will not be very significant, and if you invest too much, then you can lose a lot of money, time, and effort if the company fails. Always be comfortable with your investment decisions, and don't let anyone pressure you into investing in startups that are not a good fit for you.

You may have watched shows like Dragons' Den or Shark Tank, where the investors ask for high amounts of equity in order to make it worth their while. This is mainly due to taking an active role helping the founders and the fact that having any of these sharks or dragons in the cap table is usually a valuable asset in itself. However, the equity amounts that you will have access to for a typical angel investment check are not substantial, so don't expect to own the company!

Your investment strategy

Your investment strategy defines how many companies you will invest in at a time and how much money will be invested into each company. There are two distinct strategies that we have seen: Investing in multiple companies or investing in one company at a time. You can also decide whether these investments should be of the same size or different sizes based on the risk level of that particular startup and how much you like it. Many investors choose to start with one or two investments in their first year and see what happens with them before making any decisions on scaling this up further. You can also decide what kind of companies these investments will go into based on their apparent risk level.

As our ambassador Dan Scheinman would say:

> *But in my world, there's basically only two strategies as an angel investor that makes sense. Focus and concentrate and choose a few things, or what they call spray and pray. Because you just don't know. Either strategy is somewhat rational saying, I'm going to do a lot of deals, and I'm just gonna put a little amount of money into them. I've opted for the first strategy, I'm going to focus on a few things."*

After you have decided to move forward, the next step will be to find the right companies for you to invest in. This is arguably the most difficult part of angel investing, as it involves common sense, a deep knowledge of a particular industry, or simply, futurology. In case you are not an expert in predicting future trends, needs, and products, the best way to find good founders and good startups is by networking and making yourself known to the entrepreneurial community and the investment community. Finding the first good deals will be hard, but as you develop your skills and become a reference in the market, many opportunities will knock on your door. Your experience, in this case, will determine where you invest and where you don't.

Meeting startup founders and other angel investors

We believe that it is important to network in order to build your experience, knowledge, and assets. This doesn't really mean networking freely with anybody that pops around. Although that always is recommended, to get access to the best deals and build a name, you will need to be focused, as time is limited and precious. It's great if you can have a target of meetings; for example, you could do twenty meetings of 30 minutes a week, and this would take you 10 hours of your week, as a professional angel. Half this if you are doing this part-time.

Ultimately, what we encourage is for networking to become both an enjoyable experience and a valuable one. As you meet like-minded people and discuss topics that are interesting to you, your use of time will be enjoyed. Think of it as meeting some of your favorite people, colleagues, or friends for a chat. It must feel natural and relaxed. Don't try to make the process into a super-efficient use of time with a strict agenda and time frames, as this will not benefit the process of relationship building. And don't get discouraged if many of the meetings seem useless or a waste of time. Many relationships take years to develop, and if you meet founders or angels or VCs that do not necessarily have anything interesting for you today, they may well call you in the future with more attractive information or startups.

However, meeting people also needs to be valuable, so you want to ensure that whenever you are meeting them, you are learning something relevant to your career or your investment path. Ask questions that will allow you to build up your technical and soft skills. And also, make sure that you add value to the people you meet by giving them relevant information and advice if you can offer any. Needless to say, networking is a two-way street, and many angels have the view of giving first.

Starting out

As a new angel, you want to start meeting both angels and founders. The angels can teach you things and share their deal flow, and the founders will share deals that you can invest in. When you initiate or accept meetings, you will need to have a clear idea of what is in it for you and what is in it for them. We would suggest blocking 30 minutes for the meeting, with a view of cutting the meeting short in case there are no opportunities to be worked on and a view to set up further meetings if you find a great fit.

We also suggest that you do some preparation ahead of each meeting. Research their online profile, whether this is on Linkedin, Crunchbase, Angellist, or Pitchbook. For founders, have a look at where they worked and how long they've been entrepreneurs for. For investors, see if you can research what investments they have made. It is also useful to look people up in Google News to see if they have been featured in the media. There are tons of ways you can find information about the people you meet but keep an open mind when the information is not what you expected it to be.

As you start out meeting people, you will develop a feel for the typical topics that are covered. Generally, meetings start with a bit of small talk, where you can learn about how others interact and find out things that you have in common.

A good way to start practicing is by using Zoom or any other online conference tools. You get to do video conferences from the comfort of your own home, with no need to commute or invest too much time. We will shortly deal with how you find people; there are many ways of doing this. Money on its own attracts attention, and as you build your profile, you will attract people for better reasons too.

When starting a meeting, you might start by asking questions about their work arrangements, whether they have an office, how long they have been working in their current occupation, where they live, and maybe find things in common such as the university they attended or the field they studied.

You can then progress to the main topic of the meeting. You would normally go through a pitch deck when meeting a founder, and it is very useful to read the pitch deck before meeting them so that you can have your questions ready to fire (we will deal more with how to prepare for meeting founders in Section Four). When meeting other angels, the agenda is a bit more open, and a good way to add value is to have a couple of companies that you think might be interesting to them, as you want to add value to them. They may even give you their opinion of them if they understand the industry.

Bill Morrow gave us his view on the best source of pipeline:

 Social media, it's cool, but it's mostly noise, it's mostly talk. I think you need to pick your market place. There's nothing that beats your private network where your private network knows what you're doing. Universities spin offs, talk to them individually and tell them that you're actually looking to get directly involved with businesses from a mentoring perspective, and an investment perspective. Secondly, if you like a business and you're mentoring them, it naturally comes about that when they're looking for cash and they ask you that question, which all good founders will ask. Do you know anybody who might be interested to invest in our business? And you've seen the metrics, never mind asking them for the metrics, doesn't mean doing the due diligence. You've maybe even prepared the pack that's going to go out."

Where to meet people

Let's move on now to different places where you might meet people.

At startup events

If you want to meet startup founders, then you should attend startup events. You can find several events where startups pitch, for example: startup grind events or Angel's Den. Find events around you and go there to meet some startup founders and angels. This will allow you to pick up some business cards, sip a few drinks, and meet some interesting people. One amazing event for startups is Startup Weekends, hosted by Techstars. In the words of our ambassador David Cohen, co-founder at Techstars:

One of the assets we have are these startup weekends. So again, we have this high velocity event that happens about 1000 times a year. So any given weekend, it's happening in 20 places. That's an easy way for us to put you in the context of mentorship and have you help out and get to know the community where you are. That's often how it starts. With great reviews, you end up being invited to mentor an accelerator somewhere as well. So, we love working with people that are interested in angel investing and who want to get back to the community and mentor. And the core value that Techstars has is called Give First, which is really just a belief that we have that if you're helpful, especially to entrepreneurs, and you're not looking for anything specific in return, that you will get a lot more than you expect back in return from the community. We can help people who are interested in mentoring, connect opportunities with high potential startups, and our startup weekends are in our accelerators around the world. And you have to come at it with the attitude of I just want to help and you're not being paid to do that and not getting anything specific back. But that network will then generate opportunities to invest for you, or maybe find your next CEO opportunity or something like that. It gives back in unexpected ways. So, just reach out and we can plug you into that network. It's very, very open."

At an accelerator program, incubator, or accelerator

You might be wondering what the difference is between these offerings. Our ambassador Jason Seats from Techstars explains this gracefully:

 These words sometimes are used interchangeably. So you may find people who will use different labels for these things. So at Techstars, we run startup accelerators. And then we also do investing after our companies graduate from accelerators. Accelerator for us is about being time bound and cohort driven. So we'll invest in 10 companies all at once, and then we'll put them through a three month experience. It's like a boot camp. It's very intense. We surrounded them with mentors and tried to coach these founders on how to build their business by connecting with people who have built businesses and build businesses similar to their businesses. It's about transferring experience and experiential learning.

And the whole point is it's in the words acceleration, the goal of our efforts is to change the trajectory of the business over that three month period. They'd be a highly engaged investor in the company after they leave that sort of contained realm. An incubator, in contrast, doesn't tend to have a class concept. There's not a bunch of companies all coming in at once, every company is on an individual track, they'll join into a space. Incubators are almost always connected to real estate. There'll be support and services and things available to them.

But it's more a la-carte and the entrepreneur will step into the experience and choose the things that seem helpful to them. And they're navigating their own journey and they can hang out there, potentially indefinitely and maybe a year or two goes by and they've grown their business to the next phase and move on. I view the incubator as being a slower sort of activity and it's less intense, and more potentially customised. So they are self-driven by the entrepreneur versus accelerators are more time bound, and there's a pressure to make some progress and figure something out and you have a peer group.

A studio is something halfway in between an accelerator and a venture capital firm. And so what you should picture there is the sorts of people that may start a venture firm who also have entrepreneurial experience. Will raise some money or with their own money put together a platform where they are evaluating business ideas themselves, they are creating macro theses themselves, the firm is. When they come up with an interesting idea, they will build the first product and they will assemble a team around that product. And then they will spin that thing out into the wild. And they will go and raise capital for it, retain a major ownership position for the studio. And then attract outside capital. And then at that point, it starts to look like a typical startup out in the wild, but it's potentially at a slightly later stage and typically it has the overhang of the ownership that they hold."

There are many accelerator and incubator programs all around the world, such as TechStars, 500 Startups, StartupBootcamp, AngelPad, Seedcamp, to name a few. Although some of these provide initial funding for startups, they are always keen to showcase their companies looking for investors that can follow through investing in these companies, so it's always good to look at working with accelerators, contributing your experiences, and attending their showcase events.

It is incredibly easy to connect with these programs, even though it might seem a bit intimidating, as there is a learning curve in understanding the acronyms and language used around them. When you visit these spaces, they can be chaotic, with lots of youngsters running around from one place to another.

You can contact one of these programs and offer yourself as a mentor, showcasing your experience and feedback for their startups, with no strings attached. By helping the startup, you also get to evaluate them. The founders will have their guard down, as you are part of the same team, so you will really see how they take feedback and how resilient they can be. In case you really like them, you can then surprise them and offer to invest. If you decide to pass, which is the most likely scenario, you will have given them some valuable feedback along the way.

In this respect, David Cohen adds:

Yeah, it is easy if you just reach out to us [Techstars] on our contact form. One of the assets we have are these startup weekends. So again, we have this high velocity event that happens about 1000 times a year. So any given weekend, it's happening in 20 places. That's an easy way for us to put you in the context of mentorship and have you help out and get to know the community where you are. That's often how it starts. With great reviews, you end up being invited to mentor an accelerator somewhere as well. So, we love working with people that are interested in angel investing and who want to get back to the community and mentor. And the core value that Techstars has is called Give First, which is really just a belief that we have that if you're helpful, especially to entrepreneurs, and you're not looking for anything specific in return, that you will get a lot more than you expect back in return from the community. We can help people who are interested in mentoring, connect opportunities with high potential startups, and our startup weekends are in our accelerators around the world. And you have to come at it with the attitude of I just want to help and you're not being paid to do that and not getting anything specific back. But that network will then generate opportunities to invest for you, or maybe find your next CEO opportunity or something like that.

It gives back in unexpected ways. So, just reach out and we can plug you into that network. It's very, very open."

The other great thing about accelerators is that they do a good quality filter for an angel investor. They will filter most of the bad companies or bad founders for you. This doesn't mean they won't reject some great candidates, but in general, they are quite good at filtering out the people that haven't got a great chance of making it in the startup world.

As Jason Seats puts it:

Especially when you're starting out as an angel investor, I think it is very valuable to lean on the curation ability of others that you trust, to figure out who to trust. But it's filtering that universe down so that you're just looking at the set of things that someone else thinks are interesting. That's a better starting point, if your goal is to first learn that dynamic range. Otherwise, the dynamic range is going to include lots and lots of things that just no one should probably be investing in. So at least we're eliminating those, like helping you sort of come up with a more interesting starting point."

At a business school

Business schools are a great source of startup founders. If you have done an MBA yourself, there will usually be entrepreneurship groups and alumni working on interesting startups. Business school alumni can prove to be a great source of deal flow, especially if you can connect with Ivy League business schools.

If you haven't had the good fortune to attend a good business school and are also craving some knowledge, a good idea is to register for a short course there, which will allow you to become alumni or give access to some of the alumni networks. Most top universities are offering these types of courses for under $5,000. For example, Harvard offers an Entrepreneurship Essentials online course for $1,050, so there is plenty to research and take advantage of. We do also recommend enlisting in offline courses, as these provide plenty of networking opportunities. They are sometimes more expensive but will deliver great connections and friends in a short period of time.

At conferences/Meetup groups

Another great way to meet angels in an informal setting is by going to conferences or Meetup events. If you want to go to a conference, make sure you have a list of potential investors or founders at the conference before going there so that you can look them up beforehand. Many conferences are organized by the type of investment, so you don't go to random ones that are not interesting to you. If you are interested in Fintech, for example, there are many smaller and more targeted fintech conferences (such as lending conferences, retail banking, etc.).

Also, Meetup has more than one million people registered in over 800 groups spread worldwide.

LinkedIn

We would recommend LinkedIn as a great way to meet other angel investors and startup founders. You can search for other angel investors on LinkedIn by using the search function. LinkedIn makes it easy to connect with people in the same ecosystem and niches that you are interested in with their filter functionalities.

Some individuals will class themselves as angel investors in their profiles, and others will list their angel investments in their work experience. People that have a full-time day job can be more interesting than full-time angel investors, as they show they are still being highly productive. When you find good people, you might also want to check what other individuals also browse related to this profile, as you might find others.

It is also good to connect to groups that are interested in angel investing, especially for a given geography or linked to a business school that you attended.

Although we believe LinkedIn is a great tool, do take into consideration that many people receive tons of invitations to "network" on LinkedIn. So the best way to get someone's attention is to have a direct or indirect link to that person, otherwise risking never getting a response. Links may come from people you two know or from common interests. You may have also studied together without knowing or have similar views on a particular issue. Regardless of the links, try to get introductions or make the invites as personal and tailored as possible to maximize your response rate.

In any case, there will be many people that do not reply to your messages, so if the person is or seems to be the person you are after for any particular reason, just keep trying.

You can also grab interesting names from AngelList and look them up on LinkedIn, which is easier to connect.

However, one word of advice about LinkedIn, from our ambassador Bill Morrow:

> *My heartfelt advice, as you guys have mentioned, LinkedIn is a really useful tool. But my advice is, do not call yourself an investor on LinkedIn. Because I got 1300 direct messages in two days. You don't want to be calling yourself an investor. I mean, you are a mentor, you are somebody that can add value to the ecosystem but unless you want a whole world of pain and a whole world of really bad deals coming your way.*
>
> *LinkedIn is the most valuable tool for professional promulgation, actually getting the word out there. Facebook just doesn't figure. I think there's a time and a place for Twitter as well. But for Twitter, in my humble opinion, it would be about promoting your skills into the niche, into the sector, into*

the geography that you're all about. Once again, just a tip, I wouldn't necessarily go calling yourself an investor."

Adding value to startups as an angel investor:

We will talk more about life as an angel investor in Section Eight, but adding value and not just money is an integral part of angel investing. It is common knowledge that startup founders need money. However, as an angel investor, you have to make sure that you bring more value than just money to the table.

Let's read what our ambassador Bill Morrow has got to say on this topic:

The number one thing that investors are actually able to bring to the business and which has the biggest impact on the business is their time, their mentorship, their experience and their contacts. So, money is not a rare commodity, you can get money from everywhere. And I think the number of crowdfunding platforms that are opening up across the world, they show you that money is an important part of it, but it's certainly not the essential part. The part that's needed is actually helping run the business itself in terms of actually how to exit or how to look after their cash or contacts, should they want to move into another market, then that's going to be really important. It's the kind of value that money itself cannot buy."

Let's look in more details how angels can be valuable partners to startups in the following ways:

Sales expertise

The startup has a great idea and good product or service, but it can't get traction in the market or raise enough money. As an angel investor, you can help them by bringing your business development experience and connections to the table. You might have industry connections, a network of potential customers, or a connection to a channel for sales that is more effective. You may be an expert in SaaS models such as our ambassador Dan Martell and know how to bundle the product properly, create the perfect sales funnel, or tailor the best pricing strategy for them.

Strategic Advice

The startup has a good product or service, but they are not getting enough traction and need to make some changes. As an angel investor, you can help them with your strategic insights and advice. This may be product management experience, logistics experience, operations experience, or any other thing that can get the company moving in a more slick way.

Professional Advice

It may be that the startup does not need any money, but they are struggling with hiring decisions or other operational decisions or knowing what is the best way to scale up. As an angel investor, you can help them with your professional advice and contacts in the industry that they can benefit from. You might have industry contacts that can be helpful to them, or you may have good ideas about how to tackle certain problems in their business operations. This type of advice will be more valuable if you have worked or are already investing in other companies and if they are asking for your advice on how to do something similar in their company.

Industry Insight

Sometimes startups will just want advice on how to do something better within their industry, for example, how to do a better job at customer support or how customers perceive their brand or product.

Introductions

The startup has no money, but they have a great idea, and they are looking to raise funds. As an angel investor, you can open doors for them by introducing other angel investors or VCs. You might know other investors who might be interested in listening to their pitch, or you might be able to introduce them to some potential customers who can see the potential of the product. This can be especially true if you decide to concentrate on a specific geography or topic, and you start co-investing with other friends and colleagues. It is often said that angel investors are vital for the startup's survival until the next funding round, so introductions may play a key role in completing the next funding round faster and more efficiently.

Introductions are also very valuable in getting the startup's products to market or connecting them to important decision-makers in a relevant industry or company. Getting key contracts for needed tech, parts, or software not available to all or having a platform promote their product are all issues where the angels may provide good contacts that go beyond fundraising.

Creating your angel profile

Your angel profile is a description of your investor's professional background. You should point out relevant achievements and assets that can be useful for companies, things that make you attractive.

Some people call it an angel CV. Its purpose is to position yourself as a legitimate and credible person in front of potential startup founders looking to raise funds. It is also a way for other people investing in the same fundraising round to get to know your expertise and abilities to add value to the company. It all becomes part of a virtuous cycle.

Your angel profile can live in different places. It should be short, straightforward, and relevant. The angel market is very competitive. Investors who cannot communicate their experience clearly are unlikely to be successful in this type of investment venture, so you'll end up investing in the leftovers. No matter how many deals you see, if the good deals are turning you down, or you don't get to see the good ones, you will only end up having a poor choice. A bit like going to a restaurant, if you go to a bad one, it doesn't matter how many dishes they have on the menu, you probably won't find a really good one. However, if you go to a Michelin-starred restaurant, and there is just one option on the menu, you still know you will get something pretty special.

The main places where investors publish their profiles are AngelList (Angel.co), LinkedIn, Crunchbase, and PitchBook. Some of these networks allow investors to link their investments they have made to their profiles, so startup founders can compile lists of people investing in a specific field.

Many angels have their own websites too, where they can add as much or as little information on their investments as they want. Please note that failures are also a vital part of the information angels share, especially when they learn specific issues on why the startups or themselves as angels failed. These personal web pages are also very useful for investors to share their views on any topic and also gain a following of their own. You can check here some of our ambassadors: Martin Varsavsky, Eneko Knörr, Fabrice Grinda.

What are some key items that should be included in an angel CV? Here are a few:

Companies you have invested in

If you have invested in startups, the companies should be listed.

List the company name and the size of your initial investment. This is a good way to demonstrate your value and credibility as an investor. You can also list the post-investment performance of each company if you have that available. You might want to show how much you made on each investment or lost, if any. However, keep in mind that this information might not be that useful to other investors when they are trying to evaluate your credibility.

If you are just starting, do not despair, as all angels have been in your position at some point, probably when online information was not as readily available. You, therefore, would need to highlight other aspects of your investment or business career.

Investment background

List any investment experience you have had so far as an investor, even if it is limited. Syndicate and crowdfunding investing counts as investing, so you can list the companies you invested in through a syndicate too. This information gives you an edge over other investors who have no experience at all or limited experience with startup investing. It shows that you are willing to learn and grow as an investor and eager to gain new skills for this area of business investment. It also shows potential business partners and startups that you are qualified enough to invest in them despite a lack of experience, which reduces the risk for them as well.

Exits or successful investments

This is very important information for any potential business partner or startup founder because it demonstrates that your investment helped add value to the company so much that it was sold for a higher price than it was worth when you first invested.

Relevant professional work experience

List any experience you have had working at major companies, especially if you have held senior roles. This gives your potential business partners and investors the impression that you can work with and add value to larger companies. It also demonstrates that you are well connected with other senior individuals.

Relevant education

List your educational background and any degrees you've earned or accredited certifications. Having a degree or certification shows that you are qualified enough to learn about certain topics, such as investing in startups and business management, and able to communicate your knowledge effectively. Include the specific field of study for each degree or certification if possible. For example, if you have an MBA from Harvard University in finance, this will demonstrate that you have a high level of education in finance and investment-related topics, which is important since these skills are vital to investing successfully. The more advanced degrees and certifications, the better – so don't hesitate to list them all! Higher education also relates directly with networks, so people will know what your networks are and if they can help in securing introductions.

Extracurricular activities

List any relevant hobbies or extracurricular activities that show off your leadership abilities or general knowledge about a certain topic. Examples might be creating your own charity, being on the board of directors for a local non-profit, or writing for a blog. This information demonstrates that you have a passion for helping others and are willing to use your time and money to do so. It also demonstrates that you are interested in learning about different topics and being involved with the community around you. This is important since your reputation as an investor will be based on your community involvement and ability to help others.

If extra-curricular activities are directly linked to the industries or markets that you are interested in, be sure to include them too. For example, if you are an avid LOL player and have a deep interest in online gaming or e-sports, be sure to highlight these, even though they may seem irrelevant. There are huge industries that are completely new to experienced investors but are nonetheless growing exponentially, so younger, less experienced people may add a lot of value.

Startup experience

If you have any experience working with startups, list it in your profile under this subheading. Include any companies you have worked with in this manner, even if you were an employee instead of an investor. List the company name, your position, and the amount of time you spent working with them. This information shows that you are familiar with startups and understand how they operate, which is important to investors who want to invest in a company. If possible, list the startup's performance after you left or were no longer involved with it. This demonstrates that your work had a positive effect on the company's performance after you left or were not involved in day-to-day operations anymore.

If you have been a mentor directly or through an accelerator program, or a director or advisor of the companies, this adds huge value too and can provide sources of reference for founders at a later stage or for other investors trying to find out who you are.

Investment thesis or sweet spot

You may hear other angels talking about it, and you might be asked by founders about your investment thesis. This pairs up with your angel profile nicely. An investment thesis is a well-defined, reasoned argument on why you believe a specific investment will outperform the market or other similar investments.

As Francisco Coronel would put it:

An investment thesis is the explanation of a particular investment strategy based on analysis, research, and logical way of thinking. In the venture capital world, a general partner or what we call GP, prepares a formal document, which is an investment thesis to show other potential investors If they want to put money in the fund that these GPs are organising. I think that creating an investment thesis is a good exercise for angel investors. Visionary skills are quite important and making an interpretation of market dynamics is key. I like the Carlota Perez thesis. She said that based on historical appreciation, every technological revolution is co-related to changes in market dynamics."

It's extremely common in Silicon Valley to see equally smart firms picking very different outcomes. These range from passing on a deal to offering a wide range of term sheets. These disparities boil down to each venture firm's investment thesis — the internal rules that guide the partnership's investment decisions. Every form of investor should possess a form of investment thesis. It's what guides their philosophy in investing, which involves a wide aspect of parameters. Any good investment firm will invariably have an internal language that they use to communicate with each other about possible investments with some degree of precision. It's an indication of having a fairly precise and fine-grained sense of what one seeks. We will dig into this in detail in our portfolio management chapter ahead.

How to market yourself as an angel

If you thought that marketing yourself as an angel was not necessary, you were wrong. You will have to market yourself if you want to be a part of the angel network. The first step is to get your name out there. Make sure people know who you are and what your interests are. If you do not have a blog or any other presence online, you might want to set one up.

Eneko Knörr shares:

 Building your brand takes time. So it's not something that you can do overnight. And I mean so you have to work every day, like following people, adding content. So doing things that are in the books like it's a textbook so you have to do a lot of things that you have to get more followers and begin to get more and more interactions. So personal brand is super important because as I said, at the end of the day, you have to get in, in order to get the best deals. You have to be friends of the best investors in your country. Or your city. And you have to be friends with the best entrepreneurs. It's really the way to get into the best deals. And people have to show up. For me, I think it's an interesting strategy, that you share your experience, you share your expertise, you give tips to entrepreneurs and investors. And then they watch your videos and they say, oh, look, I really like this guy. So I want this guy to be my investor, because he's going to help me. Also, you know, he's been in Silicon Valley. So he's been doing business in Asia. So he knows a lot of these things. So I really want this guy to be my investor. So that's why I'm very active on social networks and very active networking. And I go to entrepreneurs, or I used to go to entrepreneurship live events."

The reason why you need to establish a presence online is that you will be able to reach a lot of people at once. Being well-known or marketed will gain you access to the best deals.

When you first start, if you are in the market for a great deal, you will most likely find it online. Deals do not just pop up on your doorstep. You will need to search for them, and the best place to look is online. This is why you need to have a presence online so that people know who you are and what you are looking for.

However, the hottest investment opportunities do not even make it online until they are too popular, and their valuations are way too high for any angel. You will have to be on the lookout for these opportunities as well within your extended network.

Online and offline self-marketing

You can establish a presence both online and offline to market yourself as an angel. This can help you reach as many people as possible. If you are well-known online, chances are that people will know about your investments, but the money that you raise will also come from offline connections.

You need to be able to reach out to everyone and give them a chance to work with you or invest in your opportunities. Offline connections can also help, especially if you can appear in media, such as radio, magazines, conferences, or TV. Think that Marc Cuban has gained a lot of popularity by appearing on Shark Tank.

Marketing yourself goes hand in hand with networking, so they can be considered as one and the same thing. Networking would be on a more personal or one-to-one basis, whereas we will talk about self-marketing on a more extensive scale basis. Let's look at the top ways to market yourself online:

A personal blog

Many angel investors enjoy posting online about their life, their interests, and their investments, the books they read, etc. You can certainly do the same and see how your following grows. Make sure that your writing style is efficient and easy to understand. And talk about the things that you are interested in investing in and your passions. If you would like some inspiration, you can check the blogs of Brad Feld, Jason Calacanis, Christoph Janz, Martin Varsavsky, Tim Keane, and Naval Ravikant, and Fabrice Grinda.

Social media pages

Having a presence in social media is another great way for you to market yourself as an angel. You can use this medium to present yourself as well as your investment interests. Twitter allows you to fire interesting articles or thoughts quickly. Retweets will quickly distribute your ideas. LinkedIn allows you to write articles where you can express and share your opinions. This will also help you gain more followers, which can help spread the word about your business or investment interests. There are many people on Twitter, LinkedIn, and it is useful to add your angel buddies to a group so that you can interact with their activity, liking what they write, and staying in touch.

Other social media platforms such as Facebook, Instagram, or TikTok may have slightly different audiences, but they can easily replicate the content you post elsewhere, so they are worth considering too. Angels like Dan Martell are keen users of social media platforms, and they would surprise you as he has more than 500,000 followers on TikTok!

Angel directories

There are many directories online that list angel investors and their investment preferences, deal size, amount of money they are looking for in investments, and other details that might come in handy when looking for investors. These can also help you see what type of connections you already have with other angels online, which might lead to opportunities that appear online but have no interest from any investors. Angel.co is probably the largest angel network online and a key place where you should build your profile.

On the other hand, there are always ways that you can market yourself **offline:**

Startup events

There are a lot of startup events that you can attend and listen to pitches as a judge. You can also look for other opportunities to invest in or even be an advisor or mentor to other entrepreneurs. These types of events will also help you establish your investment interests and your brand as an angel investor.

Angel investing clubs

You can also join or create a local angel club, which will help you meet like-minded people who have the same interests as you do and potentially in the same city or area you are based. There are already existing clubs that you can join, but if there is none near where you live, then it might be a good idea to start one yourself, even if it is an online club at first. This will not only allow you to meet like-minded people who have the same interests as you do, but it will also help grow your network of investors and opportunities.

What is your angel sweet spot?

In business, there is a lot of talk about your **"sweet spot"** or **"niche"**. But what exactly does this mean for angel investors?

A sweet spot or niche is the place where you can be most effective and most satisfied at the same time. It is where your interests, abilities, and ambitions align. If you have had an extensive career in one area, and it is an area you love, then this will be your sweet spot or niche.

The sweet spot for an angel investor can be ideally in many aspects, which varies on an individual basis.

Sector/industry/geography

Many angel investors are passionate about a particular industry and enjoy working with companies in that industry. For example, an angel investor passionate about the Internet may be more interested in SaaS companies. Dan Martell, one of our ambassadors at Angel Investor School, has a deep passion and has decided to become one of the best coaches and investors in SaaS companies. He now leads and is truly successful in scaling and growing SaaS companies, and the best founders and entrepreneurs go to him directly in this niche.

Geography may also be a key driver of the niche you choose. For example, some angels believe that it is very hard to get to know a specific country if you don't have boots on the ground or if you have not worked or invested in the region before.

As Zach George puts it:

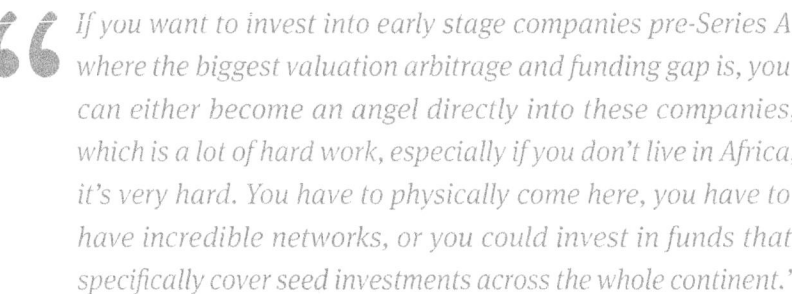

If you want to invest into early stage companies pre-Series A where the biggest valuation arbitrage and funding gap is, you can either become an angel directly into these companies, which is a lot of hard work, especially if you don't live in Africa, it's very hard. You have to physically come here, you have to have incredible networks, or you could invest in funds that specifically cover seed investments across the whole continent."

Although knowing the region is not a prerequisite, and you may have deep interests in a region that you don't know, aiming for a region familiar to you will likely mean that this is where your network and connections will give you access to the best startups. Diving into a completely unfamiliar territory will make it harder for you to source the best deals and demand a considerable amount of time and money. It will likely turn into a very steep and expensive learning curve, so think about the region and geography before investing.

Stage of the company

There are many stages at which a company can seek funding. Angel investors interested in helping companies seeking venture capital funding may focus on angel investments that will help bridge the gap between an entrepreneur's initial raise and a VC round. Other angel investors may focus on later-stage startups that have received some venture capital investment but need more to grow and scale effectively.

Angel investors interested in investing in companies at the start of their life cycle (e.g., a new startup) may focus on identifying companies with a unique idea but need funding to get off the ground. They may also focus on helping those companies get traction and help them to develop a path toward profitability. Angel investors interested in later-stage companies may be more focused on helping those companies scale and grow effectively.

Stage of financing

The stages for an early-stage company seeking financing include (but are not limited to): seed or pre-seed, series A, series B, series C, and beyond, all the way to IPO. Although most angels focus on the early stages, this doesn't mean that they can't keep adding value (and investments) to companies by following through and keeping board positions. The timeframes for each of these stages can vary widely depending on the type of funding and company seeking funding. An angel investor who is most interested in helping companies raise series A or series B rounds may spend most of his/her time working on deal flow for those rounds. An angel investor focused on pre-seed or seed deals will spend more time building relationships with potential founders and learning about their ideas to determine if their business fits well with the angel's interests and abilities.

Investment size

Some angel investors are interested in investing small amounts of capital (e.g., $20,000 or less) and others are interested in investing larger amounts (e.g., $1 million or more). This may be a function of the angel's financial situation, access to capital, appetite for risk, and tolerance for deal flow, as well as the stage or financing round of the startup.

Investment type

There are many different types of investments an angel investor can make, including ones that are debt-based or equity-based. We will touch on this subject in detail in Section Five. Angel investors interested in debt-based investments may be more interested in lending money to companies that need a bridge loan or other type of credit facility. Angel investors interested in investing equity may be more focused on helping companies raise equity financing rounds. Typically, angels will invest money and receive equity or shares, but there are exceptions where convertible notes offer interest or dividends. This will depend on individual deals.

What is really important, no matter what sector you choose to specialize in, is to keep educating yourself. As Bill Morrow states:

There's going to be a niche, there's going to be a stage, there's going to be geography, there's going to be an actual sector niche that you can concentrate on. Just go and meet these people. Unless the money is burning a hole in your pocket, get yourself educated. And if you think you know everything about our marketplace, then you're going to lose a lot of money in that marketplace. There's always time for you to be educating, schooling yourself in the particular field that you're into. Hang out at the incubators. And as I've said, it's not about being an investor if you think it's all about making money, and it's going to be an ego trip for you. You're probably going to lose,

90% of startups fail and 90% of startups fail because of their attitude, or a pretty crap company with your 500,000 euros added to it is just going to be a richer, pretty crap company. It just means it's going to take it longer to actually go out of business, than it should do in the marketplace."

Online networks

The following online resources can be helpful as you build your network:

AngelInvestorSchool.com: The biggest global investor school. Annually organizes free virtual summits bringing together the top angel investors of the world. Angel Investor School also offers bespoke 1:1 training, intensive angel programs, and online training, as well as valuable resources for initiating angel investors. There is also an active social media group to share and exchange ideas and an active LinkedIn page to post ideas and comments.

AngelList: AngelList is the largest online angel network in the world. Created in 2010, the platform has a mission to democratize the investment process and help startups with their challenges in fundraising and talent.

AngelList Syndicates: If you want to learn more about angel investing, you can find experienced investors who will syndicate with you on AngelList. Some of the best angel investors and startup founders in the world have their own syndicates on AngelList

SyndicateRoom: Invest in UK early-stage companies as a part of a fund delivered by our ambassador Tom Britton.

TechCrunch Startup Battlefield: TechCrunch is an online publication for new technology companies and startup businesses. They organize competitions called Startup Battlefield, where you can network with other startups.

Meetup: Meetup is a platform for networking with people who have common interests. Find a meetup group in your city and attend events to meet entrepreneurs, investors, and mentors interested in startups. It has become very popular for angels to set up their groups without having to invest in technology.

Startup Communities: An experiment by our ambassador Brad Feld, the app uses Mighty Networks technology and allows people to discuss startups, investing, and a big range of topics. Watch out for the Angel Investor School channel.

Startup Weekend: Startup Weekend is an event organized by entrepreneurs to help kickstart early-stage companies. You can participate as a team member or mentor during the event. It's a great place to network with other entrepreneurs, investors, and mentors in your city or region. You can register as a volunteer here too.

Crunchbase: Crunchbase is a database of tech companies, people, investors, and events. It's a great source of information on startups and their founders, investors, and competitors.

PitchBook: Another database with lots of information on startups and investors of different sizes. Requires a paid subscription that can be quite expensive for angel investors.

Generating deal flow

Deal flow is the lifeblood of an angel investor. If, as an angel, you lack new investment opportunities, you will not get access to the best opportunities. Networking is an art, not a science. It's a critical skill that must be done intentionally and decisively. Thus, an efficient network can resolve most issues regarding deal flow. You need to see a lot of deals; some angels even recommend investing in 1 out of 100 deals. This doesn't mean you need to interview 100 companies, as you can start by ruling out all of the pitch decks you receive based on how well they fit with your investment thesis.

Try to leverage your network: If you have angel investor friends, ask them about their deal flow and maybe try investing with them

Leverage social media: Set yourself up as an investor in LinkedIn and write some content there. Candidates will start approaching you directly.

Try syndication: We will talk a lot more about syndication in its own chapter. For now, you need to know that a syndicate is a group of angel investors that pool their money together in order to invest into the same startup. While investing in a few syndicate deals, you will find that you are investing with other individuals. This can act as an ice breaker to start a relationship and begin sharing deal flow.

Try online investment sites: AngelInvestorNetwork has listed thousands of startups looking for funding, and you can pick by industry and by deal size. You may also check out websites like Kickstarter and Product Hunt and approach companies you love directly.

Many of our ambassadors have stressed that networking is one of the most important aspects of angel investing. We will quote some below to share what experienced angels think:

Joo Seng Wong: *"Firstly, get plugged into the network. That is the hardest thing to do. You have to be one of the people that startup founders are reaching out to, there must be a way to find you through a mass of anonymous faces."*

Brad Feld: *"And finally, and most importantly, really work hard to broaden your networks so that you get exposed to lots of different kinds of things versus just be insular with people you know."*

Dan Scheinman: *"I think is super important that you make sure as an angel investor that you have relationships with more investors further down the value chain."*

Ullas Naik: *"You need to then insinuate yourself into the entrepreneurial ecosystem, where the best deal making or the best entrepreneurial ideas for that space are emerging."*

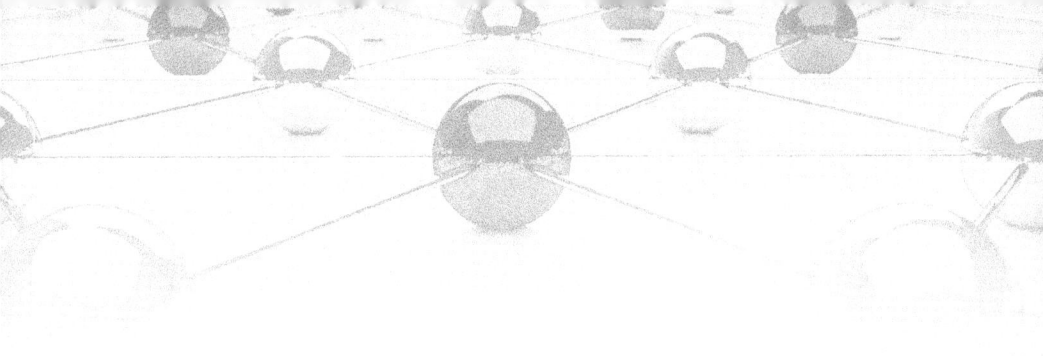

SECTION THREE

Startup Basics

In this section, we will explain what a startup is and the different business models and fundraising rounds they usually go through. For some, these terms are very confusing so let's go through each of them.

A startup is an emerging business trying to solve a problem or address an opportunity in the most efficient and economical way possible. Some of the common characteristics of a startup are the following.

It is an early-stage company that has not yet reached maturity. It does not (or may not) have a proven business model. It may or may not have revenues. It is a company that has not yet reached the stage where it can grow without outside help. It can also have very few employees, often just the founders at the very early stages.

More often than not, startups will have a business model that is quite different from that of a traditional brick-and-mortar company and may require multiple rounds of funding to optimize their business model and scale to a profitable level.

Startup culture

The startup culture (the people, the places, the lingo) is a unique and specialized culture that's unlike any other. Nothing to do with the culture of big corporates, where there is high specialism, bureaucracy, and many different roles. The startup culture borrows a lot from other fields, like business, arts, and entertainment.

It is important for you as an angel investor to understand this because you need to know how the founders and the team in the startup culture think and act. This will give you an edge in identifying and evaluating startups that can be successful.

Think of the startup culture as a new language. It's different from business, the arts, and entertainment, and it takes some time to learn. But it's important to learn about this culture. Understanding it will help you better know the founders and team members of the startup culture.

In the words of Joel Gascoigne, from Buffer:

There's no right or wrong with culture, it is simply a combination of the natural personality of the founding team in addition to proactive work to push the culture in a desired direction and to maintain certain values. I think to build a culture that can inspire people to want to work for you, you will want to take the time to make specific changes to shape it."

In short, when you are evaluating a startup try to get a feel for the culture inside the startup, ensuring that it is not toxic and that you share the same values as the founders.

Startup lingo

The startup ecosystem has its own language, and it's important to be familiar with it when you are engaged in angel investing. In order to be an angel investor, you should understand the terms and definitions below. We will develop several of these terms along the way.

Ramen profitable: Ramen profitability means that a company breaks even and pays for the founders' (and maybe their friends') lunches. This originated from the ramen noodles that the founders eat when their startup is just getting started.

MVP: MVP or minimum viable product is the initial version of a product. It is bare-bones and can be used to test a hypothesis. It should be able to attract paying customers.

Pivots: Pivots are changes made to the fundamental idea of a product in order to achieve success. One of the most common pivots is from an app to a web service or vice versa, or from a one-off fee to a monthly subscription basis.

Lean: Lean refers to the lean startup methodology developed by Eric Ries in his book The Lean Startup. In this methodology, startups use all available resources to test their ideas. They only develop products that have been tested and proven to work, and they only hire employees when needed. This saves both time and money, allowing startups to succeed faster than ever before (and keep the burn rate in check – more on that below).

Validation: Validation means that you have a product that meets your customers' needs. If your customers want and need your product, they will pay you for it. This is a great validation point for startup founders because it means there is enough demand for their product. This may also be referred to as product market fit.

Accelerators: Accelerators are companies that provide space, mentorship, and resources to startup founders. They're often located in the startup ecosystem of a large city.

Incubators: Incubators provide mentorships but don't typically give funding or other significant resources to startups. They also don't really take an active role in startups or make specific demands of them—they just provide a great place for startups to get started with room for growth and expansion as needed.

Bootstrap: Bootstrapping a startup means that the founders use their own money to fund the idea. They work on their idea every day and use the money they make to pay for it. This can last for years, but eventually, most successful startups need outside funding to grow.

Burn Rate: Burn rate refers to how much a business spends each month, and it is usually expressed as a percentage of how much it makes. A high burn rate will quickly drain the startup's bank account or funding from investors.

SAFE Note: The SAFE note is a popular way for startups to obtain funding. It stands for "Simple Agreement for Future Equity" (and perhaps also, Safe, Affordable, Flexible, and Easy) and describes the terms of the note.

Exit: An exit is when a company is sold or goes public. It's the end of the startup phase and usually happens when the startup has reached a certain level of success.

These are just some of the most common terms and definitions in the startup world to get you started.

The different startup funding rounds

A startup will usually start with sweat capital. In short, this means the free work that the founders will put into it to come up with the idea, study the market opportunity, create a pitch deck, create the initial MVP, etc. It is refreshing to see progress done by the founders with no capital; it speaks a lot about them. We suggest investing in founders that have already built something rather than talking about something they will build. As mentioned before, this is the bootstrapping round, and it is rare that startups generate revenues at this stage.

The next logical round is Friends and Family, followed by a preseed round (very small amount), then seed round, and on to Series A (larger amount), Series B, and so on. It is common to find startups that have gone through multiple rounds of funding. Some startups even have pre-seed rounds before a seed round. Moreover, new funding methods in the early stages are emerging, which do not necessarily fit into these categories. Crowdfunding, debt, ICOs, and other instruments are more common each day.

Starting from Series A, there is usually a lead investor that will help the startup with the fundraising and preparing the data room for the due diligence.

Let's take a look at the most common funding rounds and how much money is usually invested in each round:

Self-funding or bootstrapping, friends and family

This is the first round of financing. It is usually done by the startup founders and is usually a small amount (usually around $10k-$200k). When founders are funding on their own, it's interesting to ask how, whether this is through savings, or through debt. It is refreshing that the founders trust their money to their idea, though if they are getting into debt, this is a warning signal. The magnitude of the spend is also important; we are trying to invest in a person that doesn't overspend, someone who keeps the burn rate tight.

We usually don't recommend taking money from friends and family if you can avoid it, as it can get very messy when things go wrong or later along the company's growth. As an angel, this is a warning sign when the only funding a founder has managed is their own loved ones. This round is more focused on providing initial funding to get the startup going. The purpose of this round is to cover the initial costs to build a minimum viable product (MVP) and start testing the product market fit.

Pre-seed round

Pre-seed funding is possibly the first round after the founders have run out of money (or decided they didn't want to take any more risk with their own capital). The goals of pre-seed funding are similar to the friends and family round and are essentially to develop (or keep developing) the concept (product or service), perform preliminary market research and product viability, develop their pitch, get their mission and vision aligned, and create or develop a MVP.

Institutional and professional capital from venture capital firms is usually scarce at this point. The main participants of pre-seed funding will therefore be still friends and families from the founders, as well as angel investors. These may provide anywhere from $10,000 to over $500,000 in early funding. In certain jurisdictions like the UK, there are strong government incentives at this stage, which are designed for investors to reduce their risk.

Don't expect the startup to have much in terms of revenue but do check the valuations (if they have them) carefully, especially when it comes to assumptions and where they think they will spend your cash. Pre-seed stage will provide the lowest valuations for any startup and hence increase the equity you receive for your money. At the same time, risk is at its highest since there are too many uncertainties. Anyone investing in the pre-seed stage must love the founders and potentially the idea.

Finally, VCs may be interested in some pre-seed rounds for small amounts of money in order to track a certain founder or startup. Although the investment will be small and perhaps tiny compared to their usual investments, becoming a shareholder early allows them to follow on if the startup proves successful and perhaps keep VC competition away in later stages.

US Benchmark (SaaS)	Pre-seed	Seed	Series A	Series A	Series C
Type of investor	FFF, angels	Angels, angel groups, Small and micro VCs	Super Angels, VCs, Family Offices	VC, FO and PE	VCs & Strategic Corporations
Funds raising range	$200 – $500k	$500k – $2.5m	$5m – $12m	$10m – $40m	+ $50m
Valuation	$1m – $3m	$2m – $6m	$10m – $40m	$30m – $200m	+ $200m
Expected revenue	$0	$0 – $50k monthly	$100 – $250k monthly	$400k – $1.2m monthly	+ $200m

Accelerator / incubator funding

Some startups are accepted into programs that offer them office space, coaching, and funds to get started in exchange for some equity, typically 10% of the firm. A startup can get up to $150,000, mostly to cover founders' expenses and some extras for developing their first product. Unicorns like Airbnb, Stripe, Dropbox, Canva, Udemy, Grab, Zenefits, Sendgrid, and Remitly all came out of these programs. It is a positive sign to see a firm that has gone through one of the best-known incubators such as Techstars, Y Combinator, or

500 Startups. However, you may have to be careful if startups have gone through too many programs and have not been able to scale or execute their idea or product.

Seed round

This is usually the next round of financing after the funding we looked at above. Seed rounds are usually between $500,000 to $1.5 million, which might seem like a lot, but in reality, it's not that much when you consider that they have already raised money before. The purpose of this round is to continue developing their product and start with customer validation (i.e., start getting customers, revenue, etc.). This is the stage where VCs start to get interested.

Seed stage is where funding rounds become more formal. Although the startup is still at the idea stage (with potential revenues), founders find themselves trying to convince investors (and clients) that their idea or product is worth what they say it is. Startup accelerators will get involved at this stage and provide tools and some cash, but most importantly, a badge or seal of approval, which will be of great value as investors get some assurance of the quality of the founders.

Angel investors will also be key at this stage, especially those who usually wait for the idea or products to be slightly more developed (and less of a gamble) than in the pre-seed stage. As a new angel, seed stage will usually provide a lower degree of risk than pre-seed (and an increased valuation too). But it is still a very high risk for any investor. You will also see smaller and micro VC companies and the odd large VC looking to get their foot in the door (as mentioned above) in order to have preference rights in further rounds, should the startup make it.

Main goals for the funds at this stage are extending the market research, demographics, putting a team in place with clear roles, hiring, increasing marketing, and developing the product or the MVP.

Some people can raise a seed round without going to previous rounds. This is the case of serial entrepreneurs that have been able to sell their startups before. Or people that have managed to build something very unique and are well connected in the Angel / VC world.

Bridge rounds (a.k.a. pre-Series A round)

As the name states, this is a round that is in between other rounds. It mainly means that the founders have underestimated the amount of funds or time needed to complete their milestones from the previous round. Founders may also want to push the next funding round in case some major milestones are about to be reached (and therefore, valuations will be higher).

The other typical reason founders will use bridge rounds is to "survive" a current temporary or unexpected problem or situation, which should not affect the fundamental value of the startup. This may help the startup and avoid it going out of business, something none of its investors would probably want (and therefore, they are the most likely institutions or people to provide the bridges). If a bridge is not successful, founders might need to recur to a downround, where they decide to put the valuation of the company down, or sell shares at the same valuation with some preferential terms (i.e. an option to buy some extra shares after some time at a very low price).

Bridge financing may also take the form of a loan, which may be provided by banks, other institutions, or the current investors in a startup. Basically, this type of funding may not imply granting equity (and therefore, some people don't consider it as a funding round) but offers instead an interest payment and a maturity date. As its name suggests, the loan will help the founders arrive from their current point to the next funding round. Hence the word "bridge".

Moreover, the investors in a bridge round may be those that have invested in the previous round, which are faced with the dilemma on whether to invest on the bridge or maybe lose all of their money or risk a lower valuation in the next round.

We recommend analysing clearly what has changed since the previous round, what the entrepreneurs have learned from their experience. You need to decide whether you still trust the product and the founders before deciding to invest again.

It's important when investing in a bridge to check the valuation of the company. If the value has increased, you need to ask why the valuation is higher now. In a bridge, the investor generally has the advantage in terms of negotiating power, so try to get a better deal than what you got in the seed round.

Series A

This round of financing for a startup usually happens between $2 million-$15 million (depending on different factors and the geography). The purpose of Series A is for startups to expand their operations and grow their business so they can reach break-even and generate some profits. The investors expect returns at this stage, so they will put pressure on startups to perform well in order to maximize their investment returns. If they don't see the results they are looking for, they will not invest in the next round.

At this stage, you will typically see a venture capital firm stepping in to lead the round and establish governance inside the company's board by getting one of the partners to join the board. The CEO's job will have shifted to preparing for these board meetings, and they will be a lot more conditioned by the pressure of the VC. Angels sometimes get an option to invest in these rounds, though VCs many times try to keep as many shares for themselves. If you get a chance (and can afford) to follow on your investment in a Series A, try to make sure you get pro-rata rights, which means try to keep the percentage that you got in the company stable. This may require signing a pro-rata rights agreement on your previous deal.

Series B

This is usually the fourth round of financing for a startup and usually happens between $7-$10 million. The purpose of Series B is for startups to reach maturity and start generating enough cash to sustain operations. They should have already reached break-even at this stage, so their goal is to optimize their business model and grow as much as possible, with international expansion a likely event.

Series C

This is usually one of the last rounds of funding and happens between $20-$100 million. There may still be Series D, E, F, etc., before the company goes public, but the goals will not differ. This is where Private Equity firms will be seen and where VCs start demanding a higher return on their investment in order to pay off their debts (i.e., other investments they have made). At this stage, startups will be expected to generate large profits, but that doesn't mean there aren't investors willing to fund them if they are generating enough cash flow and have a good business model (i.e., sustainable). Many investors find value in Series C funding because it allows them to take an active role in the company's growth. It enables them to make sure that their investment will pay off, rather than just sitting back and collecting their returns when the company goes public.

It's important to note that the above are just general guidelines. Some startups have raised more or less funding at each stage (i.e., they have gone through a series B round after raising a series A). The key is to ensure that the amount of money raised at each round of funding is enough to reach their goal.

What is clear is that investing in startups can be complicated, and it's important to know what you are getting yourself into before investing. As an angel, you are going to invest in seed rounds, bridge rounds, and Series A rounds. After that, it is the time to start considering when to sell.

Oversubscribed rounds

In some cases, a startup will attract more capital than they need. In this case, they will divide the round into two or more tranches, each with a different price to reward investors who invest early and take on greater risk.

For example, if a startup raises a $1 million seed round at a pre-money valuation of $4 million, they may decide to follow up the seed round with a $1.5 million tranche at a pre-money valuation of $6.5 million.

There are other cases whereby startups decide to oversubscribe a round. In this case, the startup may have a high valuation for whatever reason, and they want to raise capital on a larger pre-money valuation, so they raise more capital than they need.

Startups that are oversubscribed might be getting ahead of themselves – particularly if it is their first round of funding. In the best-case scenario, it could be the case that the company has a great set of metrics, and investors are desperate to invest. In the worst-case scenario, it could be a sign that the startup is full of over-optimistic founders who are in need of some reality checks.

Always try to look at oversubscribed rounds with a healthy dose of skepticism – especially if it is the first round of funding.

As an angel investor, the best way to handle oversubscribed rounds is to try to get as much information from the startup about the following points:

What changed since the last round? What is the company's traction?

How many additional customers or users are they acquiring monthly? Are they seeing strong unit growth and user growth?

Are they profitable or close to it in any of those time periods? Are there any expenses that are being deferred until later in order to preserve short-term cash flow and keep the company out of debt – or do they have money left over at each stage of their growth curve. The last question is incredibly important. If a startup has been growing quickly, it is possible they have enough cash left over from previous rounds and/or a positive cash flow, so they can continue to grow without raising additional capital. If this is happening, you don't want to be investing in that round. You want to be investing in a round where there are no other investors who will dilute your ownership stake.

You should also be asking for proof of the revenue forecast and proof of unit growth, user growth, and other metrics from the startup. Once you have these numbers, you can decide whether you want to invest in the round.

If they have a good set of metrics, then it may be worth investing in that oversubscribed round. However, if they don't have a good set of metrics or if their traction or growth rate isn't projected to be strong enough to warrant such a high valuation, then it may be better to wait until they raise another round at a lower valuation – if that is an option.

These are all questions you want to ask as an angel investor. You should take each new round where you have the possibility of investing more or the possibility of selling as a new startup and a new due diligence. The company has likely changed massively since your investment, so be sure to check all issues thoroughly, even if you have kept in contact with the startup regularly.

Going public

The final liquidity event will typically mean the exit for any remaining angel investors, although some may wish to keep their shares in many cases, as has our ambassador Dan Scheinman with his investment in Zoom. We are talking about the hope for the company (or now Unicorn) to go public.

In the last few years, we have seen that many tech companies choose a direct listing over an IPO. The main difference between them is that the IPOs will generally have a fully underwritten issuance of shares (and vesting period for employees and shareholders), while direct listings use no intermediaries and have no guarantees on placement and allow everyone to sell their shares directly at any time. The message sent by a company offering a direct listing is strong, as it gives its shareholders the freedom to sell, meaning that the company believes in its strength and doesn't need to keep people at bay. This usually implies much lower banker's fees.

Moreover, direct listings usually avoid many of the steps of traditional IPOs, such as setting an initial price, going on extensive roadshows, and engaging many investment banks. Direct listings are usually done by well-known brands which can afford to self-market and gain interest on their shares.

In any of these cases, your shares will become liquid to trade in the open market, and provided you have invested early, you should be able to realize a good profit.

Investing in startups vs. investing in the public market:

As an investor, you should be aware of the differences between investing in public companies and investing in private companies. These asset classes differ in timescales, as for private companies, your payback is typically long-term with very low liquidity. Furthermore, private investing is more exclusive, as you need to find your own deal flow rather than just picking the stock of your choice. In addition, private markets lack public and regulated information about the companies that you are investing in. Finally, returns in stock markets can be around 7-15% per annum, while in private markets, there is a huge variance.

In public markets, you hope to buy a stock at a good price and sell it later for a higher price. You are not concerned with the ups and downs of the company. You are not bound to that company for any period of time, but the investment could be sold in an instant if you choose; the level of liquidity is really high.

In private markets, you hope to buy at a good price and develop an understanding with the company, whether it be through an employee, board of directors, or other investors. You hope to sell your shares at some point in time but will not be able to sell them as easily as on a stock market. There is little liquidity in private market investments; therefore, should you need cash quickly, there is no place for buyers and sellers to meet unless they find each other on their own. This has developed recently as a few platforms are now offering secondary markets for private shares. We are talking of Forge, EquityZen, Seedrs, Sharespost, etc. Although these platforms offer some liquidity, the market is not large enough nor liquid enough, and the fees and commissions are relatively high.

Depending on the deal structure you choose, you could be making a long-term investment in a company but put yourself in a situation where you must wait for your investment to pay off. It's not uncommon for this to take years, if not decades.

Here are some examples of what we are talking about.

For example, let's say that you decided to invest in an early-stage company, let's say Facebook. You make an investment of $500,000 and commit to a deal where if the company is sold for $1 billion or more, you will receive a significant portion of the proceeds. In this case, your investment is for a long-term gain, and you are not looking for liquidity anytime soon. Let's say your investment was made in 2004 when Facebook was just starting out and was valued at $250 million. You would have been happy with the 10% ownership stake at that valuation but instead got nothing because the company wasn't sold until years later for billions of dollars.

In addition to long-term value creation being hard with private companies, there is also no guarantee that an investor will ever get their money back from a private investment or even sell at any price as liquidity is scarce.

In contrast, in the public market, there is a liquid market where you can sell your shares at any time and at very reasonable fees and spreads. If you decide to sell your shares, there will always be a buyer for them. In addition, you can buy and sell a company's stock throughout the day. Therefore, if you need to sell some or all of your holdings in Google, no matter how much they are worth at the time, and even if there is no buyer for your remaining shares, you could instantly sell all of them on the open market. There would be no delay in getting your cash back with this type of investment.

Finally, when an investor picks a company in private markets, they do not have voting rights for that company. Often there is one vote per share owned; therefore, if an investor has 10% ownership, then they have one vote while someone with 1% ownership has one vote as well. This will vary from startup to startup and will depend on the individual case. But this can leave an investor feeling "powerless" when decisions must be made or investments are being made by the management team who may not value long-term stakeholders as much as short-term gains from investors looking to flip their shares quickly or move on after making some money. Negotiating the terms may seem like the way to go in case you invest 10% of the value of a company, something that you will likely be able to enforce. In contrast, public companies have a much more democratic process with voting rights and all shareholders having a say in how the company will be run. There is no negotiating here, and all shareholders get a pro-rata voting right as per their shareholding, and as per the rules of the exchange they trade in.

These are just a few examples of some of the differences between public and private market investing. There are many other nuances to the differences that I won't get into here; however, it is important to understand these fundamental differences before getting too deep into private market investments.

In summary, if you want to take on more risk in order to potentially receive higher returns or if you have the time and money needed to wait for those returns, then investing in private markets could be the right path for you. However, if you are looking for a good return on your investment but want liquidity, public information, and voting rights with your investment, then public markets may be a better fit for you.

Return multiples available

Making money in the angel investor world is not linked to the rollercoaster of the stock market. The stock market can crash, and this doesn't need to have a relationship to your private investments (although it may have an impact in the short term as no company is likely free from systemic risk). As an angel investor, you need to know what multiples you can achieve. With any investment, you want to make sure you can get your money back at least. If you believe in the company and plan to hold your investment for a long time, then different multiples will be available to you.

Given that angel investors invest in private companies, the average expected return multiples are higher than public companies. Some research done suggests that an average annual of 27% is available for angels investing in a diversified portfolio of startups, according to Wiltbank and Boeker.

People tend to think of a 90% failure rate for startups; however, looking in more detail, it feels like the failure rate is around 60% after six years of operation, according to Phillips and Kirchhoff.

The reality is that with startups failing at quite a high rate, you need to diversify in order to find and invest in those companies that will render 10x, 50x, 100x, or even 1000x and cover all the losses in the other companies. We have a spreadsheet available at Angel Investor School for you to test and calculate returns based on investment size and diversification.

How to establish a valuation at an early stage startup

Without a track record, there is no way to know how much a company is worth. Sure, you can put a valuation on the company based on the number of users or customers – but that will not be an accurate valuation.

Our ambassador Paloma Cabello reflects on this:

Many times you just cannot value a company. Even trying to run a valuation exercise is nonsense. You have nothing to work with in order to pull together a proper valuation exercise. So it is silly that you try to, for example, perform a discounted cash flow model of a startup that nobody knows, if it's going to exist in six months' time. Because for that you need projections

So that's the reason why many accelerators for example, if they agree to invest in a company, they have this kind of established valuation, which is that whatever startup that I think that could make sense, the valuation will be $2 million. I'm talking about companies that are likely to have or that are aiming for success in our global market or in a big enough market. So, $2 million is like the typical valuation used in accelerators. But how much do you want the equity of these companies? Depending on who you are, but if the valuation is 2 million and you want 10% you will need to invest 200k."

You will never be able to know the true value until you have sold the company or exit. Yes, it is possible that in five years, the company could be worth 10 million dollars, and you could sell your shares. But don't count on it. Even if they have brought in $2 million in revenue from your customers, that doesn't mean the company is worth $2 million – because it isn't.

The best way to figure out how much a startup is worth as an angel investor, look at the different companies in the different regions, the stage of investment, the revenues (if any), and the comparable companies in the same segment or market. These values will always be an approximation, and platforms such as Seedlegals, AngelList, Carta, Crunchbase, and PitchBook gather enough data in order to get rough but accurate estimates. In any case, we will give a rough rule of thumb of how to value a very early-stage company.

Alejandro Cremades, an expert in startup valuation and one of our ambassadors, puts it the following way:

> I think that you need to take a look at what the trends are because I think that valuing a business is an art. And I think that if you're not a sophisticated person with numbers, or maybe like you have some experience on leading rounds and thinking like that. I think that maybe you want to like to be part of a syndicate, be part of a group that is really investing in the company or maybe like to be a follower. Meaning that there's another lead that is sophisticated, and then for you to come in, so that's a good way to learn. But in terms of really valuing companies, I think that the best approach is really to understand what the market is paying. So for example, if you grab this company, and you take a look at what the competitors have been doing.
>
> In terms of let's say, it's a Series A, and it's company Y, then you take a look at what the direct competitor of company X, and direct competitor of company A in terms of pre-money valuation. Basically what you do is you try to negotiate with the founder, a number that is in between. So again, this goes back to the approach that we were suggesting in terms of having that type of partnership now. I have a little framework here that I've put together that I have in this community that I've created called the Inner Circle. People can see it on alejandrocremades.

com where I have all types of benchmarks on valuations and things like that. Typically for a pre-seed round, these valuations that go especially we're thinking about SaaS, between one to 3 million. The capital raised is between $200 to $500,000, type of investors, friends and family, angels, then the expected monthly revenue, there's none, pre-seed. Then if you go up and you go to seed, you're raising between $500,000 to $2.5 million, valuations that range between $2 million and $6 million, the type of investors are going to be angels, micro VCs, individuals from angel groups, and so forth. And then you're going to take a look at the expectation on the monthly revenue and that's going to be between zero and $50,000 on a monthly basis. When you go to the Series A, the desired capital is going to be between five and 12 million the valuations that people are going to be looking at is going to be between 10 and 40 million.

And the investors are going to be again institutional, family offices, super angels, and people like that. The expected monthly revenue for Series A now you're seeing it between $100,000 to $250,000. So that acts as a very good framework. And then when you go to Series B, and then beyond maybe like a Series B, where you're looking at is between $10 to $40 million that the company is raising valuations between $30 million and $200 million so obviously, the range becomes a little bit bigger. And then now you're seeing VCs, family offices, private equity firms, and really the expected monthly revenue is between $400,000 and $1.2 million. So that hopefully gave a little bit of a frame of reference that the people that are listening to this can use to value all the companies that they're taking a look at."

First, to figure out how much money a startup is worth, ask yourself the valuation of other startups in the same sector. Having a benchmark of what other similar companies are worth is the best way to determine the value of your own startup.

The problem with finding a benchmark for your startup is that there may be no other startups in your sector doing exactly what you are doing. So, you need to look at similar startups in different sectors and use a benchmark. The best way to do this is to find out what similar companies have raised money at different stages and compare the valuations of those companies to your own.

You can do this by using AngelList, CrunchBase, PitchBook or just Google the company and search for "Series A", "$8 Million Series B," etc.

This is a similar process to what professional investors use when they value companies at later stage rounds of funding where there are other competitors in the same sector. It is much more common to do this with later stage valuations than at an early stage since there is plenty more information for later-stage companies in terms of financials, revenues, business models, etc., which may not be available at the beginning of a company's trading life.

The other method for valuing startups is to look at how much revenue the company is generating and then add a multiple on top of that based on the funding stage.

The problem with this method is that it can be very misleading. This is because it doesn't take into account how much money is needed to fund the company, nor does it account for the cost of acquiring customers, nor does it take into account the profit margin of the product.

For example, if you were to look at a company that has generated $500,000 in revenue with a one million dollar valuation, you might be tempted to say, "Wow! A $1 million valuation on $500,000 in revenue – this company must be worth a lot!"

But that is not entirely true. If you looked at the details of this company, you would see that they have a long runway ahead of them, and they are going to need capital to grow their business. You would also see that they are charging 5-10% margins on their products (which is very low), so all of their revenue is being spent on running the business, and there isn't much left over for profits. That means that they aren't really profitable yet. So when an investor looks at this company and sees a valuation of $10 million dollars, he is not only looking at how much money was raised during the round, but he is also looking at how much money will be needed to run the company in the future.

When you are valuing a startup, you want to look at the revenue multiple and then add whatever profit margin is required to cover the cost of running the company.

There is no exact formula for this, but it can be calculated with the revenue multiple. If we were to use this formula for our example above, we would see that even though they have $500k in revenue, if you take away their acquisition and operating costs (probably around 15% of revenue), there isn't much left over.

You can use this method when you are valuing a startup, but, as mentioned above, there is no exact formula to do this, and you will need to predict where the company is headed. You can't base future performance on past performance nor the models and estimated forecasted returns as these will never materialize as the founders have presented them in their pitch deck.

Valuation of an early-stage company is close to futurology, so trust your gut. In any case, we do recommend not fixing all discussions on the valuation of a company since the focus should be on whether or not you like the potential they present. After all, valuation ranges will be those mentioned in the table above, and if the startup succeeds, the initial valuation will simply be an anecdote to remember.

Biggest pitfalls: why startups fail

There are plenty of reasons why startups fail. As mentioned before, there are stats showing that between 60% and 90% of startups will fail. It is therefore imperative to know the main reasons why startups fail.

When analyzing a new investment, knowing the main reasons why startups fail will allow any investors to make a better decision when considering whether to invest or not. Moreover, there may be some reasons why startups fail that may be avoided or that the particular expertise of an investor may help solve or mitigate and turn a failing startup into a unicorn.

We have divided the main reasons into pre-investment and post-investment to help you understand the main reasons.

Pre-investment: No market need or demand

This is by far the biggest reason why startups fail. It's also the easiest to avoid even before starting to work on the startup. Ideally, you want to invest in something that is solving a pressing problem for a large group of people, and that it's solving it better than the current solutions on the market. If you can't answer yes to both statements, then you should consider looking for another investment opportunity.

Do also ask yourself the following:

- ✓ Does the company have customers? If not, is it because they are not interested in the product?
- ✓ What is the problem being solved?
- ✓ What is the pain being addressed?
- ✓ Is it a large enough market to be worthwhile?
- ✓ Is it scalable?
- ✓ Is the company struggling to develop customer interest?
- ✓ Solve a meaningful problem for other people
- ✓ Is the timing right for the product?

The startup needs to "make something people want". Entrepreneurs are always too confident about how easy it will be to get customers.

Pre-investment: Not the right team and/or poor execution

Perhaps even more important than the market is the team and its execution capabilities, but teams become manageable to a degree. The startup may have the right idea and the right market, but it has been poorly executed. Poor execution covers a whole host of sins from poor product design and development, being unable to sell your product or service, not having enough capital, etc. Sometimes businesses execute perfectly, but they are just too early for their market, and the timing isn't right yet. Unfortunately, timing is pretty much impossible to predict before jumping in head first, so this one can be tough to avoid without investing a huge amount of money in market research upfront – which we don't recommend doing.

Our ambassador John Colley has shared invaluable insights into having the right team:

If you're an angel investor, and you're being presented with an opportunity, ask yourself the question, are you being presented with the right team? Are there gaps? Are their weaknesses? Because at a very early stage, it's relatively easy to make changes or indeed, to increment with maybe one or two key hires, just to get the right balance of people. And it may be that the founders have maybe brought a couple of friends that don't have quite the right experience. Maybe they don't even have the right personalities. Maybe they have a gap. And they're relying on contractors or freelancers to do something really critical, maybe a core piece of coding, which is something that the whole project is going to have to rely on down the road.

What if that Freelancer is no longer available or disappears and there's a problem with the coding then they're in real trouble.

Another part of the team that you've got to look at is how well balanced is the team in terms of personalities. I mean, I've worked with a lot of founding teams, and classically the lead founder, the CEO, tends to have a pretty strong personality. And if that personality is not being reined in a little bit, he / she is not working as a real team member with other teams, the whole thing can really get pulled in a direction that maybe it shouldn›t go. So you've got to apply some common sense. But you've also got to apply a little bit of experience. And now, look at the people in front of you and say, Is this the right combination? And ask them, because if you look at the team, and you say, okay, they're brilliant at building the product, but, you know, maybe they're not going to focus, right. So they might be poor at strategy, or they might have a really great product, but they can't build it on time or to the right quality. So they're poor at execution. Or simply, there's this issue.

There's an old saying in this game, A player's hire A players, but B players hire C players, and that's because other B players don't want to work for B players. So they're poor at team building, you have to really be critical and go in with your eyes open and ask yourself, have they got the right combination of people? And I would add just to this, that if it's just a one man team, then you really got to do some serious thinking about either you don't invest, or you go and help him put a team together because it takes on average, and this is a stat that I've looked up, but it's, they're saying 3.6 times longer to outgrow the startup phase if you're a solopreneur, as opposed to being a team. So as an investor, you could be putting a lot more money in before you make progress, it was just a one man band. So yeah, the team is pretty critical."

Pre-investment: Product (Un)friendliness

The startup needs to build what the users want, not what they think they need. And they need to make it easy to use, fun to use, something users want to come back for and pay for.

If possible, ask the question and try to spend some time with early adopters to get their feedback. Try to use the product or MVP yourself. Try it out and play with it. This will allow you to understand it, understand the usefulness, and its ease of use. It will also help you give the founders valuable feedback, whether you invest in them or not.

If the business is pre-sales, find out more about who the leads are and what their feedback to the product or service is.

Pre-investment: Poor product / service / business model

This happens when the market wants something for a certain price, but you're selling it for less or giving it away for free. It also happens when you have a great product or service, but there isn't enough demand and no way to make a profit, so you run out of money and can't raise more without pivoting either business model or product/service offering.

Never trust the old phrase: If we build it, they will come! There are two potential scenarios here. They will or they will not. Maybe the startup is creating a new market, but you need to be careful and analyze why the product was not needed before (or why there was no market for it before) and why there would be a market today.

Ask yourself and the startup:

✓ How is the product going to make money?

✓ Who is going to buy it and why?

✓ How much for?

- ✓ Can the business move from free to paid?
- ✓ Can the product scale?
- ✓ Is there a compelling use for the product or service, or is it just a clever technology or idea?
- ✓ Can you find a scalable way to acquire customers?
- ✓ Can you then monetize them at a significantly higher level than your cost of acquisition?

The Cost of Acquisition (CAC) must be significantly lower than the lifetime value (LTV) of a customer. Ideally, it should recover the CAC in under 12 months. There are many metrics, which we will discuss, but be sure to include as many as you can in your assessment and due diligence.

Pre-investment: Legal issues, challenges, and setbacks

Make sure in your pre-investment due diligence you check to see if there are any legal issues outstanding. Sounds like a no-brainer, and in some instances, at a very early stage, there is not much to check. But the product or idea may be based on a patent or a certain code that is pending approval or is in litigation. These are huge red flags that may or may not have a solution.

Legal challenges are very expensive to handle, and when they come from a major competitor who has the firepower to drag your startup through the courts, this should be considered. These challenges may emerge later, and the best response may be to retreat and pivot rather than stand and fight. Also, keep in mind that these big players may be the perfect partner in the future or the perfect company to acquire the startup's tech, so don't rule a startup without the proper analysis.

Pre-investment: Passion

Founders are the heart and soul of the startup. So are they passionate about the business? Do they (happily) bore you with the idea? What are the founders main motivations behind the startup? Is it money? Do founders have a day-job? Have they invested their own money? Have they left everything behind to build this?

Be careful of the wrong motivation or lack of passion. Founders will clearly show when they are fully into the startup. Move away if they are not.

Pre-investment: Lack of investor interest down the line

One of the key factors for a startup to succeed is to "survive" through multiple rounds of financing. So before you invest as an angel, look ahead to anticipate how the investors in Seed, Series A, Series B, and beyond will respond.

- ✓ What are the major trends?
- ✓ How competitive is the space?
- ✓ What comparative deals can you identify?
- ✓ Has the train already left the station?
- ✓ Who are the likely Series A investors?
- ✓ Have any particular VC funds invested in similar companies or competitors?
- ✓ Is this a geographic issue?
- ✓ Has a competitor already claimed the space?

If a major competitor has already done a large capital raise, they may have the resources/investors to win at any cost! And if there are certain companies who have struggled with financing, why is that?

Also, bear in mind that specific VCs that invest in a particular space may have already placed their bets on a competitor and may not want or may not be allowed to invest in any competition. Therefore, if any of these funds are key for the startup's fundraising down the line, there may be challenges if there are no suitable replacements or backers.

Pre-investment: Sector-specific issues

Some sectors have specific issues innate to their business models. As an angel, it is somewhat advisable that you invest where you know the market or the sector, as this will allow you to contribute to solving the problem and also that you know about the certain pain point.

For example:

- √ Software companies can get tied up in their tech and issues with customer development and market fit.
- √ Social media startups can struggle for traction and come across problems developing a viable business model.
- √ Or Mobile Apps may have no clear route to a sustainable business model.
- √ The music industry has changed radically in the past few years and has always come across technical and legal challenges.

So think about what your sector expertise is and where you will focus. Be sure to check our section and session on developing an investment thesis!

Startups can also fail for external reasons. Some of these can be looked at before you invest, but many will come up after the early stage. We have divided them into external and internal.

The reasons below would assume that you have already rolled the dice. Now it will be up to you as an angel to try to help founders in sorting out these challenges, even if they are external to the startup.

Post investment external: Get beaten by competition

You always have to keep your eyes open for the competition – don't assume that first-mover advantage is enough to win. If the startup initiated a great product or service, it will stimulate many imitators, and you need to keep an eye on what they are up to. Many will copy the business in other jurisdictions (where the startup intends to scale) or even in the same markets.

When you meet founders who say that "no one else is doing this," be very careful. Even if no one is doing this NOW, they may soon copy the startup or may have been developing it for some time.

If you have placed your bet as an angel investor, keep a wary eye out for the other players around the table and encourage the founders and team to do the same. Never get complacent, even if your product is the best (today).

Post investment external: Product mistimed

This is related to execution but goes beyond just being too early for your market. It's when your market is ready for what you're offering, but your business isn't ready yet, or you don't have enough capital to get started or grow fast enough to meet customer demand.

Another way this happens is if you're trying to do something that hasn't been done before and you need more time than normal for customers to catch up with your way of doing things or figure out how they want it done instead of how they've been doing it for years. This usually happens when someone has a great idea but hasn't spent as much time learning about their market as they should have before starting their business, so they haven't figured out how their customers like to do business yet.

- ✓ What if the available technology is not ready for your product?
- ✓ Are you dependent on other markets or other products developing to be successful? AI? VR?
- ✓ Does the startup team have tunnel vision and is failing to see the obvious? Are they spending enough time talking to customers?
- ✓ Are they ignoring feedback?
- ✓ Premature Scaling – the more a company grows, the further away from profitability it becomes
- ✓ Scaling, hiring, funded, growth – 70% scale too early – too much too soon

Regarding the timing for scaling, the startup is not ready to scale when:

- ✓ They don't know the LTV of a customer
- ✓ The business is not acquiring customers in a repeatable way
- ✓ Spending more time in the business than on the business

There can be other issues around timing:

- ✓ Problem/Solution Fit – who is your customer, and what are you solving for them
- ✓ Product/Market Fit – create enough demand to scale into your market

✓ Channel Fit – lower customer acquisition cost and increase revenue to reach profit

Timing and execution is certainly a place where you can help as an angel.

Post investment external: Tough geographic expansion

Location has to be congruent with growth. For example, a large installed base in New York may not guarantee take up in San Francisco or London. Does the business scale outside of its locality?

Remote teams could also be an issue with challenges for teamwork, communication, and cooperation.

Below we discuss the main internal reasons why a startup may fail. We have divided them into Operational, Management, and Financial issues. All of them are important and deal with specific issues common to most startups.

Post investment internal: Pricing & cost mismanagement

✓ Is the price high enough to cover costs?

✓ And is it low enough to scale?

✓ How is the cost management equation?

✓ What is the runway like?

✓ What is the burn rate?

✓ Can they survive the winter?

✓ What are the product/service price assumptions? Are these being realized early on?

✓ Is there a better way to price the product or service, which will be easier for customers to understand while still bringing in sufficient cash for the business?

As an angel, you need to spend time understanding the cash flow and break-even forecasts.

Post investment internal: Lousy or no-marketing

If you know the market as an angel, you can help the startup focus in the right direction.

- ✓ Is the product getting the right attention?
- ✓ Are they converting leads to sales?
- ✓ Evangelise the product or service?
- ✓ But what if the team are all coders and tech-stars who love building the product but don't know how to sell it?
- ✓ Do they have enough traction?

As an angel investor, you have this outside perspective and can step in and help them to address this weakness by hiring a CMO.

Post investment internal: Ignoring customer feedback and them altogether

See no evil, hear no evil ...

- ✓ Is the team getting regular customer feedback?
- ✓ Do the new features and roadmap for the product address customer needs, or do they address the team's desire to build a funky product?
- ✓ Is tunnel vision an issue?

You need to encourage continual customer contact and feedback and get the founders out talking to customers regularly.

The truth may hurt, but failing will hurt even more.

Post investment internal: Inability to pivot / adapt quickly enough

This goes along with being too early for your market or having poor execution, but instead of missing the timing completely, you've gone into your business knowing that customers want things done a different way but are unable to pivot quickly enough to stay ahead of the market.

For example, you open a restaurant that serves a menu of one-of-a-kind, exotic foods but two months in, you realize that your customers prefer to eat the way they do at home instead of trying new foods. That's when you need to pivot quickly and change your offerings, and it's also part of what makes this so tough. If it takes too long to get things done or change direction, then the market has already moved on, and you're left in the dust.

Post investment internal: Lack of Focus

As the startup matures, the founding team has to deal with a range of different challenges; managing investors, dealing with employees and customers, answering to the board of investors (including angels). This might dilute their attention and, in the worst-case, will have a negative impact on the product and the customer experience.

Angels and investors have a responsibility to act as a mentor and a guide to help stop this becoming a problem. As Dan Scheinman would put it, he is often called the CFO or CHIEF FOCUS OFFICER.

Post investment internal: Disharmony among founders/team/investors

It is super important that the founders get along between themselves and with their investors. This is the ultimate partnership, and one cannot exist without the other. If any issues arise, you must spot it going in and resolve it by restricting the team.

When the disharmony occurs with an investor – and this might be the Series A investor after your round, it can mean shutdown for the company. The investor may decide to withdraw, leaving the company with no alternative other than closure. Be on your guard for any warning signs and do your best to address problems before they become critical issues.

Founders' agreements and clear-cut language on subscription documents and terms will help, but always try to have a cohesive relationship and ensure open communication between parties.

A prenup won't prevent a bad marriage ...

Post investment internal: Lack of Angel's network

This is something as an angel investor you can actively intervene to prevent. Make sure that you use your network to help your investee company. During most of our sessions, there is one key value-add that angels can add. And it's their network and connections.

Startup teams cannot do everything themselves. Be sure to open your contacts and try to get involved in the composition of the advisory board. Are there gaps? Can you help to improve it? Is there an advisory board? Would one make sense?

Too much work ... a.k.a. "Burnout."

- ✓ Overwork is a culture in a startup.
- ✓ Work-life balance is seen as a weakness.
- ✓ Having a balanced team that can share the burden is essential.
- ✓ Ability to delegate is non-negotiable.

Angel investors need to be alert to the signs this might be happening and be prepared to step in and address the issue before it becomes a critical problem.

Financial issues: Running out of cash

Clear as water, running out of cash can destroy small and large corporations, including startups. Be sure to check or ask what the story is with the burn rate, the runway, and how close are the set milestones and the next funding round.

Startups running out of cash are often a case of poor financial cash management. The management team has potentially not been addressing the next funding round soon enough.

The next funding round effectively starts as soon as the startup has closed the current one. It is like running a marathon. Don't allow the startup to pause when it comes to fundraising. It may seem amazing closing Series A, but in order to keep the engine running, founders and their close angels need to keep at it until the next round.

You need to be very aware of the cash flow, break-even, and runway in front of the business, and take active steps to ensure that the fundraising is done in a timely manner.

Respecting Milestones

Setting clear goals and milestones cannot be underestimated. Some of them can help the startup in many ways, for example:

Remove Risks	Early paid customers
Team hire	Positive feedback
Overcome tech obstacle	Product Market Fit
Prototype & MVP	Update feature set to improve gaps
Customers	Prove Business Model
Beta Test	Customers and commence scaling
Customer validation	Lower the CAC
Ship product	Successful scaling

Failure to meet milestones could lead to a reduction in valuation or a failure to raise and complete the next round at all. Cash is king, and certainly so for startups. Leaving it too late will make the startup desperate, and investors sense it and will eat your lunch.

Do check that the milestones are reasonable and that the startup is hitting them promptly. Otherwise, be sure to step in as soon as you can with constructive feedback and ways to reach them.

SECTION FOUR
Evaluating Startups

This chapter will explore the evaluation criteria for startup companies that an investor is looking to invest in. This is a very important exercise as it will shape how we approach the investment decision process and how to perform due diligence.

There are many different ways to look at this topic. We like to prioritize an approach that is based on the idea of a "rational investor" who applies a certain methodology to make investment decisions.

The reason for focusing on this approach is that it tends to be more effective in the long run than other approaches. Why? Because it enables the investor to be consistent in his approach from deal to deal, and therefore allows them to develop a methodology that makes sense and can be repeated over time, adjusting for learnings due to failures and successes.

We will discuss what you should look for when evaluating a startup, how to perform due diligence, and how you should present your findings.

As an overview or summary, you can decide on the kind of companies you want to invest in based on the following investment criteria.

Investment criteria

Founders and management team: You have to consider the founders and the management team as well as the people involved in making the product or service. Try to pick your companies on the people that run it rather than on the idea or market, as nobody can tell the future, but great teams will be able to execute almost any idea or pivot when things go bad. It's easier to tell whether a person will be successful rather than if an idea will be successful. Ask yourself whether you would buy stock in the founders if these were available. You want to invest in a startup that has a strong management team with a track record of success and ideally founders who have built something together before (or even worked together). Management should have experience and knowledge that will help them run the startup and execute plans efficiently. They also need to have a good amount of passion and drive because they must be working on their startup full-time.

As Derek Sivers puts it, ideas without execution are worth nothing.

Ideas are just a multiplier of execution

It's so funny when I hear people being so protective of ideas. (People who want me to sign an NDA to tell me the simplest idea.) To me, ideas are worth nothing unless executed. They are just a multiplier. Execution is worth millions:

Awful idea =	-1	No execution =	$1
Weak idea =	1	Weak execution =	$1,000
So-so idea =	5	So-so execution =	$10,000
Good idea =	10	Good execution =	$100,000
Great idea =	15	Great execution =	$1,000,000
Brilliant idea =	20	Brilliant execution =	$10,000,000

> To make a business, you need to multiply the two.
> The most brilliant idea, with no execution, is worth $20.
> The most brilliant idea takes great execution to be worth $20,000,000.
> That's why I don't want to hear people's ideas.
> I'm not interested until I see their execution.

The target market size: The market size is defined as what is the potential market for a particular product, service, or cause. You need to consider things like population size, number of people affected by a particular problem, income levels, and other factors to determine market size. It makes sense to rule out companies that are not looking at a big enough market as they won't be able to deliver the multiples that you are expecting. Small local companies with good revenue that solve a local problem are nice, but probably not what you should be looking for. Scaling potential needs to be a company able to achieve a valuation of $1 billion. Also, it is probably advisable to focus on tech companies, as brick and mortar companies take too long to build and are tough to scale internationally.

Market timing and penetration: This factor refers to how much of the market has been captured by competitors. If there are no competitors in a certain field or industry, this might mean that your startup might have first-mover advantage, and it could be able to capture more customers than if there were multiple competitors already working in that field. However, it might mean that they are looking at a market that is too small or immature, and its time has not come yet. For example, Xignite, an API and data provider for fintechs, had to wait for ten years until the market was ready to consume its app commercially.

Product or service: You need to consider whether you understand or are curious about the product or services being offered by a company and the problem they are targeting. Your investment will be based on how well you feel about the products or services they offer, so it is very important that you know about what they are providing and whether it is something that you would like to use yourself. If you can't use what they are offering, then it might be harder to connect with the company and the problem that they are trying to solve.

Market opportunity: You also need to look into the market's future, taking the role of a futurist. Try to predict the potential market size for this type of product or service, how many people may buy it, potential growth rate, and potential profits if things go well.

Evaluating pitch decks

The main document that startups use to present themselves to investors is the pitch deck. A deck is a presentation with slides that explain the startup, the problem that is being solved, how the problem is being solved, and other things such as the traction so far achieved. Most pitch decks are made using PowerPoint or similar tools and delivered by email. Historically, after sending the pitch decks, founders would meet with the potential investors and present the idea, answering any questions from the investors. Nowadays, many of these presentations occur online via Zoom or Teams, and there may be sessions where multiple startups are presenting to multiple investors, arranged by either an accelerator or a syndicate.

Our ambassador Laurel Touby describes a pitch deck beautifully:

> *I look at a pitch deck as a symphony. It's a musical piece. It's a structured musical piece. It's got to all fit together and you can't just have one note. So I would say, it isn't about one*

slide. It's about a bunch of slides. And they all have a way of interacting. For example, you have to have some information, of course about your market size, your competition, your team, how you're going to market the company and get customers. But if one piece is misaligned, the rest of it falls apart. For example, if you're the wrong founder trying to start a biotech company, you might have the best idea in the world."

When evaluating a startup's pitch deck, take your time and go through it carefully. As you read each slide, you should ask yourself: Are the points being made clear? Are the numbers believable? Are the assumptions reasonable? Is the startup addressing an interesting market and a complex problem? Does it seem like there's a clear path from here to success?

Don't think too much about how much money you would need to make in order to get your return on investment back (your ROI). Instead, think about whether this investment aligns with your personal interest and values and whether it would give you some kind of satisfaction or sense of accomplishment if it did well. Angel investing is more than just making money; it should be fun! If it's not fun, then you should find something else to do with your time.

While you're going through the pitch deck, make notes of anything that stood out to you, either positively or negatively, on a particular slide. Then when you've finished looking at the slide deck, go back through it and make another pass through your notes. This will allow you to see both positive and negative things in context with one another. It will also help you avoid making any decisions based on just one or two specific slides without looking at the whole pitch deck as a whole. This process is critical for basic due diligence because it forces you to evaluate all of the information in context with other information instead of taking any one piece as an isolated data point that might be misleading by itself.

Prioritizing pitch decks

Sometimes, the person that you receive the pitch deck from is as important as the pitch deck itself. As our ambassador Laurel Touby puts it:

 I will definitely respond to a lead investor who sends me a pitch deck. If it's not a lead investor, if you don't have a lead investor, I like to get it from any investor who's in your round, who is sending me a pitch deck. If it's not an investor in your round, I'd like to get it from a professional investor who knows about the space that you're tackling. Anybody who's invested in that space, any expert in that space. It could be an entrepreneur who's an expert in that space that you're tackling. So if I get a pitch deck from a successful workplace entrepreneur who says, Hey, this is something new and different, this HR tech company is doing something very original, I will take a look at that, and I will be sure to respond. And then anyone who knows me, that's the next level.

When a pitch deck comes from a trusted source, it may have been checked, or you should trust it comes from serious founders. Even if the trusted source is not investing in the company, but they still send the deck to you, it may be because it fits your thesis better. For example, if an investor who focuses solely on marketplaces forwards you a deck for a SaaS company, they may be forwarding you a great opportunity, but since it doesn't fit in their thesis, they are not allowed to invest."

Within the pitch deck, make sure you look at the following:

Problem and solution

Pitch decks usually start with the description of the company, the problem they are attacking, and the proposed solution or technology to solve it.

This part of the pitch deck should allow you to understand the actual problem if it is painful enough for people to pay for a solution, and whether the solution is a worthy one that will effectively tackle the problem. This is where you will get a lot of data about how well it's designed and how much potential it has to be successful.

Laurel Touby adds:

> *The most important thing about a problem that you're solving is that it is extremely painful financially to the customer. That's the most important one. And if it's not painful, financially, it's got to be painful in terms of time that they're losing, or some promise that you're going to solve a problem that they care about. And that can be hard to identify, but it's very, very key to having a good problem.*
>
> *When looking at a product or service in a pitch deck, you should be looking for four things: What problem is it looking to solve? What value does it offer compared to its competition? How is it better than its competition? And finally, what is the business model, and how will the startup make money with this product or service? In order to understand each of these things, you need to ask yourself lots of questions and do some independent research on your own as well. You shouldn't just take what the founders say at face value; you should look into the answers for yourself as objectively as possible."*

Market and Product Offering

Next, a deck should contain information on how big the market they are trying to address is. What is the TAM (Total Addressable Market) as well as the SAM (Strategic Addressable Market)? This can be local or global, and there may be different stages where the startup plans to tackle.

When looking at the market size, check that the founders have done a lot of research and validate by using public sources of data. Check whether founders have taken the time to do surveys, too, and that the info on the deck is not just from a 10-minute Google search. Try to check whether the founders are being honest and thoughtful. Is it a one billion-dollar market or just a 100 million dollar market with an incumbent player thriving already? If so, how are you going to tackle that?

Like our ambassador Alexander Jarvis says:

> *What matters more is the thought that goes into things and what the actual specific numbers are. And be genuinely looking for order of magnitude. So whether or not it's 670 million or 700 million. That'd be quibbling over 30 million difference. Is that number large enough? So if you say you can only invest in a market, which is a billion dollars or more, then it doesn't matter if it's 500 million or 999 million, it's still not what you're looking for. So who cares? So long as the market is large enough.*
>
> *The most superficial founder might just write like food is a $1 trillion industry, just because they actually don't really understand the industry but they saw on TechCrunch someone raised a 40 million Series A so they want to copycat the business, but they actually don't know anything about what it is they're doing. So they read that investors want to have a really big number. So they write some stupid headline number on their pitch deck, the market size, and that's it. But when you ask*

> them questions, why is it a trillion dollars? They don't actually know because they didn't spend any time thinking about it."

Think about the numbers quoted, check the sources, do your own research and apply your own experience if you know the industry.

Financials

This is a key component of any pitch deck and is where you're going to get a lot of information about whether or not the startup can survive and achieve success. Many believe that the financials are completely invented and that exponential growth is a lot of wishful thinking. But the financials will be able to detail many aspects of how the founders think, what the assumptions behind the numbers are, and what the different metrics they are using are. Numbers in the deck will always be larger than reality, and they will never materialize, but the thought process behind the numbers will give you a feel of the product, the market, and above all, the founders and the way they think and work.

The financials in a pitch deck are usually broken down into three sections: The market opportunity, the startup's value proposition, and the startup's business model. This should all be complemented by a set of assumptions made by the founders.

The market opportunity is how much money is being spent by consumers on whatever problem the startup is solving. The startup's value proposition is how much value its product or service offers compared to everything else in the market. And finally, the business model is where you'll get detailed information about how exactly the startup plans to make money from offering its product or service for this particular market opportunity.

There are several different ways that startups can make money offering their product or service for a given market opportunity, but there are roughly five main business models that most startups use:

subscription services, marketplace businesses, platforms for third-party services, freemium services, and service businesses.

According to Laurel Touby:

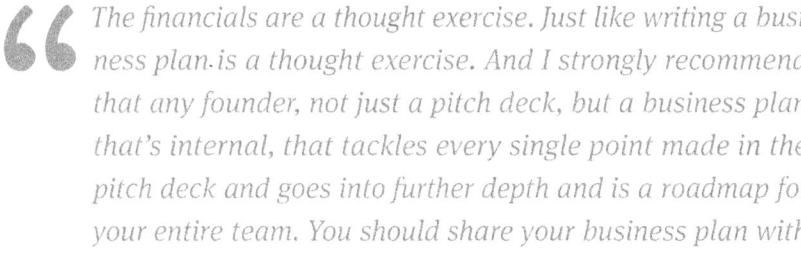 *The financials are a thought exercise. Just like writing a business plan is a thought exercise. And I strongly recommend that any founder, not just a pitch deck, but a business plan that's internal, that tackles every single point made in the pitch deck and goes into further depth and is a roadmap for your entire team. You should share your business plan with your entire team. In terms of the financials, I want to see that you've been thoughtful about it. I don't expect you to achieve these goals at all.*

When I started my company, I had sold my investors on a dream financial model that was going up and up into the right. It said I was gonna make 25 million in sales in three years, it was completely crazy. Most financials are completely crazy, but I want to see a big audacious goal that you're going after. I want to see that you're aggressive but you're realistic. So that's a fine balance to make. I want to see that the costs increase as the company moves forward. What I don't want to see is a flatline of costs that, in the early stages, you have no idea. I'd rather be much more conservative in some ways, in terms of costs, than anything else. And then most of the costs for me I care that they're human and not a cost of goods sold, office space. I don't want to see a lot of high and increasing fixed costs. So I don't want to see a lot of high fixed costs. It worries me if you have to achieve $5 million before you can even get to profitability.

I want to see that you could, if you wanted to get to profitability a lot quicker, but you have the choice. So it has to be realistic. It has to have all the costs baked in. A lot of people don't put in certain costs, like legal fees, insurance, marketing."

Team

The team section of a pitch deck is where you'll find information about the people behind the startup and how capable they are. This will just be an introduction to the key members of the team, including the founders. Despite the information on the deck, you should definitely do your research, which should include asking people you know about them, if possible.

The first thing that you should look for is whether the founders have relevant experience. If they don't, then you should ask yourself whether they've had any relevant work experience in an area that has any similarities with what they're currently trying to do. The second thing you should look for is what kind of other companies or projects the founders have worked on in the past. You want to see some kind of consistency here because it shows that their past experiences have given them some kind of expertise that will help them make their current startup successful. The third thing is how many employees the startup currently has and how many employees it hopes to have in the future. This will give you some information about how serious and competent this particular group of people is compared to other groups. It will also show indications of the burn rate and if the startup has over or under-hired people. Finally, look into each founder's personal background and try to get a sense of their personalities. Are they easygoing? How good are they at working with others? Do they work well under pressure? These kinds of things might seem silly, but they can have a big impact on a startup's success.

According to Laurel Touby:

> *So when you're looking at the deck and you're looking at the team slides, some things to note are logos. I hate when they put a picture of the founder or even an avatar picture of the founder. And then they have a list of logos underneath. And they do that like across the whole slide, they have three founders, all their logos underneath, it's the stupidest thing ever. I don't*

want to see logos, I want to see bullet points at the very least. Just bullet points of what makes this person the person to start this company right now. So, a bullet point saying like, captured 200 million, in this market in a previous company. Worked in a related field, worked at a related bigger company, something like that.

And I want to see that for every co-founder. Otherwise, this is definitely a weakness when I see just logos. I also want to be sure there is related experience. I can't tell you how important that is for the founders to have related experience in an adjacent field, or something that is relatable.

I also want to see that there's somebody technical as a co-founder on the team, because I invest in tech companies. For any type of company, you're going to need a technical co-founder because, believe it or not, everything is tech these days. There isn't one company out there right now that doesn't have some kind of tech enablement. So, I would argue that you need that for any kind of company. I like to see success and not just somebody right out of school, I want to see that they've had some kind of success in their lives in some way.

And I want to see more than just one or two people. If I see only one or two people on a slide, that gives me pause. I think you should put people down on this team slide, even if they haven't yet joined. And you should have already identified top people who you have spoken to, who are going to join your team after you raise. I want to see that you've identified who your team is going to be.

I also want to see an advisor slide. That's part of your team, your advisors, and you should have at least five advisors. People who are experts, people who are impressive. And don't just have a bunch of white guys, and a bunch of old white guys. Have a series of ranges of ages, colours, nationalities, genders, all kinds of people on your advisory board. You should not just *be white. Unless your entire company is focused on government contractors, but even government contractors have females on the other side, so I don't think you should leave gender out. So those are some of the most important things on a team slide."*

Meeting the founders

There is interesting research about how many founders a startup should have. We (and research) believe an ideal number is two, as research shows better performance by a pair than by solo founders. Moving past two founders is OK, but more than three becomes messy as it will be hard to get consensus on tough decisions, and too much equity will have to be allocated to founders to keep them in the game (too little equity will drive them away to other ventures).

Once you have shortlisted and identified the startups you may invest in, the next step is to meet the founders. The first meeting should be a get-to-know-you session where you should have plenty of questions prepared about the founders personally and the business.

Here are the things to look out for when screening founders:

Are the founders passionate about their business?

This is perhaps the most important question to ask. Can the founder speak passionately and articulately about their business? Do they tell a good story? This is crucial.

This is not to say that you should judge the founder by how well they speak. After all, you don't expect the founder to be an expert in public speaking. However, if they are unable to tell a good story about their business, then it is a clear indicator that they don't really believe in what they are doing. If the founder is very technical and cannot "sell" you the business, maybe he or she should partner up with someone who is more sales-friendly.

If a founder cannot convince you of why the business will succeed, then you need to move on. What makes sense to them might not make sense to you; however, if you don't get any positive vibes from them, then it probably isn't worth your time and money.

For our ambassador Martin Varsavsky, age will not matter, and it all boils down to motivation:

> *So, maybe the best answer would be to say that age is not a key factor in entrepreneurship, within adulthood and death or death of some mental qualities. There are some incredibly old, very successful people in business. And there's occasionally somebody incredibly young successful in business. But I think the question goes more to motivation. Do you still have the motivation? Do you still want to do these things?"*

Can the founder describe how they will make money, and is it ambitious enough?

Every startup has to make money at some point or other in its lifetime unless it is a not-for profit-organization. If a founder has no idea how their startup is going to monetize, then it probably isn't worth your time and money. The last thing you want is a high-cost startup with no obvious source of revenue. Sources of revenue and business models may change along the way, but the founders should have an initial idea of how they plan to make money when approaching investors. Great products and services which tackle tough problems are amazing and could well serve their purpose, but if the marketing or the business model fails, they will never make it past the design stage.

As our ambassador, Anthony Rose states:

> *Startup is all about having an idea, building something and then having people actually use this. And it's about establishing*

product market fit and you taking a bet. So I've got this amazing new music sharing app, will anyone want it?

What I would like to see as the investor is the confidence to know that even if the idea you're showing in the pitch deck isn't going to work, the founders are hungry to make it work. They're super opportunistic, and they're going to try different things. Use data instead of spending all my money building it, they're going to make a quick prototype and see if it works. So it's all about agile finding that use case before they've run out of money. Then I think it's about maybe the motivations of the founders. If they just want to build a business that's going to make you 100K a year in revenue, great. It's a nice gig, but maybe it needs a bit more ambition. If on the other hand, I see their deck showing that they're going to do 100 million a year in revenue by year three. Okay, great. You're a footsie 500 company, very nice; statistically unlikely. I think those figures are way too made up, there's going to be a big disconnect at some points."

Can the founder describe the product?

The product is one of the most important parts of every startup, a problem without a good solution is still a problem. The more effort and time the founder has put into developing their product, the more likely it is that their startup will succeed. If they have a mockup of their product, or if they can demo it for you, that is a really good sign.

Most startups don't have a fully functional product when they start looking for funding; however, if they have access to some sort of prototype, then that's good enough for you to get an idea (however rough) about how the product looks and works. Getting your hands on the product or service will certainly get you engaged, so it is in their best interest to have something for you to test and use, so they should make the effort.

If the founder cannot describe how their product works even after spending some time with them, then move on to the next one. There are too many great startups out there waiting to be funded; don't waste your time and money on a startup that isn't worth your attention.

When looking at the product, we suggest you follow Gokul Rajaram's advice:

 I think what you want to look for is a product that's loved and ideally is used. So you can see people using it on a very regular basis. Once you have that, I typically look to see if there is a product in the market. It's sometimes far too early to think of monetization, but you have enough models.

The primary model, especially of media companies, is that if you have people spending time in your app and service for long periods of time, you know that you can monetize it. So for example, TikTok, which is a big video app, including dance. People are spending 72 minutes a day, more than an hour a day, in the app. You know that if someone is spending 72 minutes a day, there are going to be various ways to monetize it. Similarly, a lot of SaaS services nowadays go with the freemium model, which is a release of a free version of the product. Then they monetize by upselling, some paid versions. So when I see a company, many times they don't have a paid version yet, they have a free version. What I look for is the people you're acquiring, are they using the free version without churning, and so are they being retained?

To summarise, retention and engagement are the two key things that you look for very early on. If you have retention and engagement, which means a huge percent of people that you acquire in a certain month stay on with you 12 months down the road after 24 months or under. You don't know at least 12 months, because the company's not around for 12 months.

Even the next month, if at least 80/90% people stay on, or ideally 95% of people stay on and less than 5% we will drop off, you know that there is something there. If 50% of people are dropping off every month, and you're basically half way because you acquire 100 customers, 50 of them drop off; that's not going to be a product that will be monetizable or that you can build a business on. So in the early days, the focus was on building a product with very high retention products used a lot, products loved a lot."

Is the founder transparent?

If the founder is not transparent in their dealings, then you should be skeptical about investing in their business, as you should with anyone not being honest. When you are looking to invest in a startup, you expect the founder to be open and honest about their business.

This doesn't mean you should take everything they say at face value; however, if they start making excuses for why things aren't working out or if they lie about how much money they have spent on development, then it is probably best to move on. You need to trust your gut when it comes to your investment decisions, and if your gut tells you that something is off with the founder's dealings, then don't invest in that startup.

Many of the figures and values, or even functionalities, may be exaggerated or "potential". However, it is vital that there is an open conversation about the prospects, what can go wrong, what should go right, and what the potential ways to change or fix something are. Startups are deep into the unknown, so a lot of things can go wrong. Good founders will acknowledge this openly and expect their product to be a constant fight against the unknown to make things better. So anyone trying to "sell" you that there will be no setbacks in their business is simply not worth your time.

How to evaluate a winning founder

As Dan Scheinman reminds us, the investment world can be really competitive:

 I believe that in this business, where you're competing against all sorts of funds, you're competing against all sorts of other angels, you have to have a differentiated strategy to find the bigger winners."

When it comes to building a strategy, you must first find a great founder. The first job of the founding team is to create something that other people want. The second job of the founder is to raise money from investors or customers. There are probably hundreds of thousands of things that people want, but if you can't sell them the product or service, then it's probably not worth investing in.

And when it comes to investing as an angel, you need to figure out which founders you need to back and which strategy you will employ to find them.

Here are some of the traits of a great founder.

Great founders have a "product sense"

A great founder can tell you what's wrong with an existing product. They can explain how their product is superior. And they can tell you how it will be better than everything else that's on the market. If you ask a great founder why your product will succeed, and they say, "I don't know, I just like it," then don't invest in that company. They also know where the industry is going and what they feel will drive it.

Great founders have a "market sense"

The market goes hand in hand with the product, and markets change. A great founder can tell you who their competitors are and where they are going wrong. They can also tell you who their customers will be and why they will buy your product even though there are cheaper alternatives available to them. If a founder says, "We just know we can do this better than our competitors, and our customers will come because we have the best solution on the market," this is a warning sign, as they are not thinking about their plan for getting customers.

Great founders have a "people sense"

Startups are all about culture, innovation, and sales. They need to deal with employees, customers, other founders, and, of course, investors. A great founder can tell you what they will do with each employee and how they will get certain tasks done before they start. If the founder cannot explain in detail what their hiring and training plans are, then you should be cautious. Do they understand how to hire? Can they attract good people? Great founders understand that great hires are the most important thing when it comes to building a successful company. And perhaps as important as dealing with employees, founders need to reach investors for funding and customers to buy or re-sell their products.

Great founders have a "plan sense"

A pitch deck without a business plan and someone to effectively execute is a sign of trouble. Startups need direction and a captain steering them as things change (which they inevitably will). A great founder can explain not only how they are going to achieve their goals but also why those goals are achievable and what is likely to happen if they fail. They can show you how they will achieve this and how they have planned for contingencies. If the plan seems too simple or there is no risk of failure, you should be wary. If there are no contingencies planned and the founder "will see as they go" that is also a question mark.

These are just some of the things that we look for when evaluating a great founder. But there are many more, including passion, honesty, integrity, intelligence, and humility, to name a few, which don't need much explanation.

However, it is difficult to judge these traits by just talking to a founder. You need to spend a lot of time with them and watch them work. A great founder can convince you to invest with just one meeting.

Maybe the best way to get to know a founder is to be a customer or client. If you're not a customer or client, then the next best way is to invest in people you have coached or mentored. In any case, references will add information to your decision, and as you develop experience and meet several founders, your gut instinct will develop as well. You need to be patient and structured in your approach, learning and taking notes of all that went well and all that didn't.

How to prepare for pitch meetings

When you are getting ready for investor pitches, it is great if you can spend some time preparing for the meeting. Have a good understanding of what you want and how much cash you would like to deploy. You should also have a good understanding of the different types of deals you are willing to invest in. And be ready to say no or not yet and be honest about your reasons for it too.

Here are some of the steps that you can take to prepare for pitch meetings.

Specify the purpose of your meeting with the company:

The purpose of the meeting is to determine whether a company is a good fit for you or not. You want to determine whether you should invest in the company or not. It is not a social meeting and, although the first few minutes are about chit-chat, the meeting should be focused.

This step is important as it will set the agenda and frame your questions. The agenda will determine the type of information that you are going to get from the meeting. If you have a clear idea about the purpose of your meeting, you will formulate the right questions.

Prepare the right questions:

The right questions will help you gain a good understanding of the opportunity presented to you. It will also help you get a better sense of the company's strengths and weaknesses. In addition to the financials, you should have some questions about the business model, market opportunity, team, and management.

This step is very important because you want to understand what the company is all about. If they can answer your questions clearly, then you can make an informed decision.

Here are some sample questions that will help you make an informed decision about whether this is a good company or not.

What are you doing? What are your products and services? How does it work? Who are your customers? Where do you sell your products or services? How do you make money? What are your revenues? How many customers do you have? Where is your business located? – location of the product or service, location of the customers, location of the team members. Does the company have a patent or other intellectual property? What are its growth rates? Has it been profitable in the past? Profit and loss statement. Who are your competitors? How big is the market that you are targeting?

Although it may sound obvious, when preparing the questions, you will likely be researching the issues, market, products, etc. So this will lead to more questions and a better understanding of what the market and the product are all about. Don't just base your questions on the pitch deck; take it as a starting point and try to answer the questions directly with research to then check the answers with the founders. You will find that if you are prepared about the subject, the meeting with the founders will turn to a much deeper conversation, which will end up being much more rewarding.

Also remember that founders are scrutinizing you as an angel, and if they have several investors to choose from, they will select those who seem most knowledgeable and not likely to waste their time.

Scrutinize the company's financials before the pitch:

Given that a typical investment pitch lasts less than twenty minutes, it is important that you have prepared by reading the pitch deck in advance. One of the things that you can do before the meeting is to scrutinize the company's financials. This will help to ensure that you have a good understanding of the company's past performance and future prospects.

A good way to do this is to see whether there are any red flags in the financials. For example, the fixed costs are increasing heavily as the user base grows, or if the salaries that are being paid are over the roof, you should try to get an explanation from the management.

And needless to say, the assumptions and the key metrics will be more important than the forecasted profit figures in year ten ...

Top questions for founders

There are a number of questions we like to ask a founder to get a sense of the viability of the business and the product.

It's helpful to start by looking at David Cohen's checklist

 So what I like to do, like Simon Sinek(author), I start with why. Why are you doing what you're doing? You could be doing anything. And if the answers are, well, I have a spreadsheet and it tells me that it's going to work and I'm going to get really

wealthy. To me, that's a red flag. The why of the entrepreneur has to be much deeper, it has to come from what I call intrinsic motivation, internal motivation. They have to really want to change the world in a certain way. They have to feel the pain of their customer. And so, I'm looking for that. Why are you doing this? Well, because, you know, people have this problem and they shouldn't have this problem and maybe my cousin or my mother had this problem, and I don't want to see others have it. This is an intrinsic motivation that will keep them going when it gets difficult. So I'm looking for their why first and foremost. Obviously, the skills; this is the ante to the game. You just have to have the basic skills to be able to do the thing you're doing. You wouldn't go give your car to an auto mechanic that doesn't know how to repair a car, right? So you wouldn't give your money to an entrepreneur that doesn't know how to code or build a business that they're talking about. So you're looking for the skills, and then you're really looking for the obsession with the product and the solution. You're trying to understand that this person wakes up and thinks about this. They go to sleep thinking about it. They shower, thinking about it. They eat lunch thinking about it; they're just obsessed with it. And so, it's hard to fake that. You can say I'm very passionate about this, but you can tell who's really obsessed if you spend time with them because this is what they love."

In summary, probing for skills, motivation and obsession are the key points to look for. Looking at other factors such as MBAs can help to highlight some of the skills and the potential for networking on a candidate can be useful, but never trust too much education as there isn't a clear correlation between education and success as an entrepreneur. The old joke amongst angel investors is that the way that you value a startup is very scientific. It's a million dollars for a good idea, a million dollars for an early prototype, and then you subtract half a million dollars for every MBA that's involved.

Here are some good questions to ask founders when meeting them:

Why are you the best person to build this product?

This is a simple question that is often overlooked. A person's answer to this will give you a sense of how self-aware of their skills they have. Many founders don't know what their strengths and weaknesses are, so they're unable to answer this question effectively. If a founder can't give you a good answer to this question, it means they probably don't have the right experience or skills required to build their product.

What do you think about solving the problem?

An entrepreneur will usually have an idea of how to solve the problem they are trying to solve. It is important to understand how they think about solving the problem as it will help you understand if they have thought through all aspects of the problem and solution.

What part of your product are you most excited about?

This is again an indicator of what motivates them and how passionate they are about what they do. Founders who get excited by different aspects of their product tend to be more successful than founders who only like one part of their product. For example, if a founder loves talking about their product but doesn't get excited when talking about the engineering challenges, that could be a red flag.

What is the biggest risk to your business?

This question is actually a bit of a trick question as many founders will think about a few different risks but not all the risks they should be thinking of. It is important to ask this question multiple times and get a sense of what the founder thinks are some of the risks that may impact their business. This will help you understand if they are well prepared for all possible outcomes in the future or if they are building their business with "blinders" on.

What is the worst-case scenario for your business?

Again, this is a trick question to try and understand what the founder thinks their business might look like in the future. Many founders paint a rosy picture of their business that doesn't align with reality, so you want to be sure you understand what they foresee for their business. This will help you understand if they have an overly optimistic view of their business.

What do your parents do?

You may think that asking personal questions is not allowed, but it can yield great answers. It shows what the founders think of themselves and their path.

What is the worst thing about your company? (and how are you fixing it)

This question may come as a surprise to many, but it just opens the floor for the founders to be honest and for you to understand if they believe to be "perfect" or if they are humble enough to recognize errors and figure out ways to fix them.

Top questions to ask yourself about the deal

After you have looked at the entrepreneur and been introduced to the idea, you need to evaluate the opportunity. This stage is for you to introspectively think this is the right deal for you prior to spending more time doing due diligence. Here are a few things to consider:

Is the team right?

Even if the idea isn't that good or the market is not there yet, but the team is great, that's a reason you would want to invest. If the idea is truly great and the team isn't so great, that's still a reason you may not want to invest. This is because it will be harder for the team to execute the idea. Great teams who are more adept and familiar with the market can execute faster.

In addition, if the team is capable and talented, they will be able to make pivots to the business and continue to grow if necessary.

When you are looking at the team, you need to look at the following:

- ✓ Does the team have a history of successful ventures?
- ✓ Do they have a track record for creating something from nothing?
- ✓ Do they have a track record of growing something from small to large?
- ✓ Do they have a track record of mismanaging or running a business into the ground? (if so, what were the reasons?)
- ✓ What is the team's skill set? Are they relevant to this business? Do they have the ability to execute on this business? Is their skill set relevant to what you see as the needs of the business?
- ✓ How many people are in the team? It is better to have a small number of people with complementary skills than it is to have too many people who don't know each other and don't really know how to work together. A small team can be combined with additional members if necessary, but a large team makes it harder to manage overall.

Is there a big market for this idea?

You want to make sure that there is enough money in the market for this idea that you can get a return on your investment. If there are tens of millions of potential customers, then that makes it easier for you because if you can capture one percent of that market, then you will be able to get a good return on your investment. However, if there are only hundreds or thousands of potential customers, then that makes it harder because even capturing one percent of the market is not going to give you enough money to get a good return.

Is this idea original and defensible?

If there are existing companies with similar products or services, then you want to make sure that there is enough value in the idea that those existing companies cannot easily just copy it. If you have a unique and proprietary idea, then it makes it harder for others to just copy it and steal your business. If you are an entrepreneur and are launching into a space that has already been occupied by others, then make sure they do not have the advantage of history or scale while you do not have either of these advantages. Make sure that your idea can stand on its own merit, even if someone else will see how valuable it could be.

When evaluating whether this idea is defensible, look at:

1. Is this a new concept? Does it do something different than what is already being done? Does it improve upon what is already being done in some way? Or does this just cut into something else that already exists? A new concept will make it harder for someone else to steal your business because they will have to recreate the wheel all over again, while your business will be ahead of the curve because it will already have what they are trying to create.

2. Is this idea patented? If so, it will be harder for someone else just to copy you and steal your business because you will have a legal defense with your patent. Patents are not very common in SaaS businesses, though, so no worries if there isn't one available, as this applies more to physical products.

3. Is the idea proprietary? Is there some aspect of what you are doing that is unique and cannot be easily copied? If so, then that makes it harder for someone else to copy your business and steal your market share.

Does the idea solve a problem that people want solved?

Sometimes people come up with really cool ideas that they think people need, but in reality, no one needs it. No one wants it or wants to pay money for it. You need to look at the entrepreneur's idea and determine whether other people really want this service or product or if they don't really care about what is being provided by the business and if they won't pay anything extra for this service or product if it wasn't there for them. You need to make sure that people actually do want what is being offered by the startup; otherwise, you won't get any return on your investment.

Here are a few questions to ask yourself when evaluating whether people want or need this idea:

1. Is the problem being solved something that people are complaining about, or have they been looking for a solution? If they are complaining about the problem, then that makes it easier for you to see if people will pay for a solution. It is also important to see how painful a problem is.

   If no one is complaining about the problem or looking for a solution, then you need to see whether you can create the platform or market for this idea by marketing it yourself through other media and platforms. Think about companies creating new markets, like Apple creating the smartphone, Netflix offering movie streaming, and Uber offering transportation booking on a smartphone.

2. Does the business target a vertical market, and do people in this market have money? If so, then that makes it easier for you to evaluate whether people will be willing to pay money for this product or service. However, if your business is targeting a horizontal market and anyone can use your service, then it becomes harder for you because there is easy access to a free product. You want to see whether there is enough wealth in the industry and enough demand for your product or service that you can get enough customers who will pay extra money to use it.

3. Is this a business that people want to be part of because it is cool, or is it a business that people want to be part of because they get value from it? If people don't want to be part of this business because they don't get value from it, then you need to figure out how you will be able to make them see the value and want to pay for the product or service.

4. Is the price of what you are offering competitive with the competition? If there are other similar products out there cheaper than yours, then you need to evaluate whether your product has enough additional features and benefits that make it worth the price premium over the competition. Will people pay more money for your product just because of all its cool features? Or, would they rather save money and use the competition's product instead?

How to perform due diligence

The final step before making up your mind is due diligence. This will be a deep scrutiny of all there is to know about the company.

Bear in mind that smaller, newer startups will have little for you to do due diligence on. However, it is always good to get as much data and documents as you can, even if it means signing an NDA (more on that later).

Due diligence involves many factors, and there is no "one" correct way to do it. It varies among the different startups and sectors that you are evaluating. Most important factor in due diligence is to be unbiased and resist the temptation to get emotionally involved.

Performing due diligence is not the same as selecting companies. David Cohen puts it beautifully:

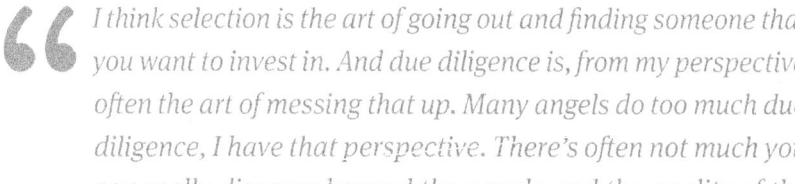

> *I think selection is the art of going out and finding someone that you want to invest in. And due diligence is, from my perspective, often the art of messing that up. Many angels do too much due diligence, I have that perspective. There's often not much you can really discover beyond the people and the quality of the people, because so much is unknown."*

The process according to David can be divided into three main parts:

Selection

This involves knowing what you are looking for. For example, you have identified a startup that you would like to invest in, but before investing in it, you will want to know if it's worth investing your money. This pre-planning involves research on the team, market, progress, and idea. In most cases, this research may lead you to conclude that the startup isn't worth investing in at all, or there may be some areas where investment makes sense.

Because we are talking about early-stage startups, there won't be a lot of information to go with. So the most important element to research is really team. As David Cohen explains:

So, team is so important that we say it three times. When you're making an early stage investment they probably don't have customers, they probably don't have a meaningful product yet or market penetration. So for team, do I believe that these people were put on this earth to do this thing? What is their intrinsic motivation? What is their unique insight? What is their drive that's going to keep them from quitting when invariably gets hard? Team, team, team. Do they have the skills and permission to do this? Were they put on this earth to do it? We really look into that. Are they good people? Next is market. Do we believe there's an opportunity in this market? Is the market shrinking? That's good. Is the market growing? That's good. Is the market static and pretty much work the same way for a long time? Could be good, but usually not as good as shrinking or growing. So, you want change as an investor, opportunity for markets change. If something is shrinking, people used to pay more money than they do now for this thing, maybe they're just missing some kind of innovation. We look at the market. Do we care about this market? Then progress. We believe that entrepreneurs actually do stuff. We don't think they just talked about doing stuff. What progress have you made? Is that progress impressive given the resources that you've had? Are you sitting around waiting for someone to fund you? Which won't be a fit for us. And finally, idea, I put it last because it's not worth much. There's no original idea really. Other people have the same idea. It's really about the team's ability to execute it. A few Bonus points if it's really novel, and it's likely to change by the way."

Due diligence

This is where you will perform all your checks on the startup and try to find all relevant information about the company (its financial standing, reputation of the management team, any legal issues, etc.). The aim here is not just to find out whether or not there are any issues with the company but also to understand what the issues are and how big they are. Also, look into the founders to make sure you are not dealing with criminals or people that have known issues. And make sure their documents are in order. Ensure you check their company formation documents and founders' agreement to cover scenarios like quitting or firing. In the financial model, check the drivers that make the company scalable and ask yourself whether they seem realistic. We have added a due diligence checklist at the end of the book for your information.

Remember to keep it relatively light, as early-stage won't allow for too much diligence anyway. As David Cohen reminds us:

We know due diligence is a great way to talk yourself out of a great investment. Airbnb, what a crazy idea. Who's going to sleep on someone else's couch? Who's going to get in a car that's not yours and be driven around by someone in an Uber? This is crazy. You can talk yourself out of it. But what if it works? And that's how you should think as an angel investor."

Post-planning

This is where you will decide if investing in the company makes sense or not. You will also plan for what you will do after investing in that company. This involves planning for exit, raising more money, product development, etc.

The process of due diligence can be very time-consuming, and depending on your approach, you may have to spend weeks or months on it if you want it to be thorough. This isn't a bad thing as long as it is worth the time and effort put into it.

Inside the due diligence process, some aspects are worth looking at with care. These include: company and sector research, legal issues evaluation, financial analysis, etc. Let's take a look at each of them now but bear in mind our ambassador Susan Preston would allocate approximately 200 hours for a standard due diligence, when others may allocate as little as two and a half hours for very early-stage startups

Susan believes that:

> *On diligence, I don't think you should outsource that. I think that's the wrong thing to do. I do feel strongly that you need to get to know a company well, in order to make an intelligent investment. And in fact, to be valuable post-investment, you really got to know the company and you do that through diligence. So I prefer my current fund, my Seachange Fund, which is a collaborative model that I can get into and discuss if you'd like. On average, collectively, for everyone that participates in diligence, we probably do about 200 hours of diligence on a company to get to the point of making a decision to recommend an investment.*
>
> *Of course, you do due diligence in stages. And you can cut it short in the process at a much earlier time. But you need to take a large macro and thinning it down to the very specific questions as you're going along and diligence so that you can make a well informed decision on your investment. And there are multiple decision points, factors and so forth that go into making a decision on investment."*

Company and Sector Research

Research on the company's business model, market position, competition, finances, etc. You should look at its current standing as well as its future plans for growth (if any).

You should also evaluate the market position of the company and its competitors. This can be done by looking at how the market is segmented, how big each segment is and what the competitors are doing in terms of marketing, pricing, etc. You should also look at what opportunities exist in that market for new entrants.

Our ambassador Anthony Rose has an interesting view:

I am always deeply sceptical when I see a pitch deck about how the company is going to build this cool stuff that they say that they've got. I'm always thinking how many people do you need to build it? Will it work? Will people want it? So for me as the investor the first thing is I'd kick the tires on whether people really want this product for testing and validation if they're done. Can they really build the products? What team have they got? Is it outsourced? Are they building more than they can build on the budget for the money they're raising?"

Legal Issues Evaluation

When evaluating a startup, you should check whether any legal issues could come up in future. For example, if you are evaluating a startup that has filed patents previously, then you should evaluate whether those patents are still valid or not (in case they have been challenged). If they have been challenged, then it is important to evaluate why it has happened. It may be because the patents were invalid, or it may be due to a patent war where an existing company is blocking new entrants into the market (this happens often).

In most cases, legal issues can be resolved without having to spend any money, but it's important to do your research here as well so that you don't get caught unawares in future. There are some other legal issues that you need to research about, but in most cases, it involves looking at financing, intellectual property, etc.

It is also important to analyse the cap tables and see who owns most of the company. You are looking for a healthy and simple cap table that rewards founders and also is forecasting for equity to go to staff.

It is also important to know where the company you are investing is incorporated and whether there are any restrictions or tax advantages. The operating company may be in your country, but the holding company will probably be in the United States, the UK, Singapore, or any other market-friendly country, which gives added protection to the investors.

Checking the shareholders' agreements and the founders' vesting of shares may also be worth your time, as you will be able to tell what happens if there is a conflict between shareholders or founders and when founders can sell their own shares.

Financial Analysis

This is an important part of due diligence and where you may spend a lot of time. It all depends on how much data is readily available. At this stage, you will be doing all sorts of financial analysis to check if the startup can generate enough cash to sustain itself in the long run or not. You will also be evaluating financial projections and forecasts, which will help you to decide whether you want to invest or not.

You can evaluate financial projections based on historical data on product sales as well as cash flow reports. You may want to evaluate the quality of financial data by using some ratios (like return on assets and equity). These ratios are also useful for comparing this company with a competitor company. And remember always to check the assumptions behind a financial model. Is the growth reasonable? Are the marketing costs increasing over time? What is the expected profit margin? Are taxes being taken into account?

Are financial models important?

Given that most early-stage startups have yet to generate significant income, it may seem odd to ask about financial models. But, if you are going to invest in a startup, you may want to know things such as how the company will make money, how much money will they make and how soon, and whether they achieve the goals in line with their growth.

Most of the well-known financial models, such as ROCE, IRR, NPV, etc., are not appropriate for early stage startups. They are useful in evaluating mature businesses with a history of profitability and know what they expect to earn over the next several years.

But for early stage startups, investors need a different kind of financial model. It's called an equity model. The goal of the equity model is to show how much money the company will make and when they will make it in a way that makes sense for early stage startups, i.e., without having a history of actual results to draw upon for guidance.

The equity model is based on two things:

The assumptions that the founders use to project their future performance and the mathematical model they use to project what those assumptions will lead to.

With an equity model, the goal is not to arrive at a precise number for projected revenue and profit. Rather, the goal is to show that the assumptions and inputs used by the founders are well-reasoned so that you can evaluate whether you believe them and whether they make sense for your investment thesis.

You should try to see an equity model before you invest in a company. If you can't get one from them, then it's a big red flag that you need to consider before making your investment decision.

Our ambassador Alex Jarvis helps a lot of founders with their modeling, which shows the importance of thinking about the business around its drivers:

So I build these big models which people have to spend a lot of time in and think through absolutely everything in the business, including the server costs when they're going to hire people, bonuses, all those things. Why? Because the numbers are absolute total bullshit garbage. All right, but just the

absolute rubbish. But what is important is the thinking that's gone into those numbers. What's happening behind them? So what I teach founders, when they get asked questions by investors, is if you do one of my models, or you do run a model, whatever, and you actually do it for yourself, is this business a good ROI on my time?"

A founder should be able to understand how income and cost drivers move in relation to things such as customer growth and attrition.

As Alex puts it:

 All right, so what do you want to ultimately get to is to be able to answer questions like, if you were to move your break even period, forward six months, how would you do that? And that involves knowing your revenue drivers, your cost drivers and understanding that marketing has a factor immediately on your cost base, but an impact on your future revenues. And so if not investing in marketing, you're not going to get those revenue targets, but your costs in the short term will be higher. So you could say, Well, look, we're currently raising a million dollars right now, under that assumption, assuming our CAC is $30 and I hire seven people in an18 month period, we think we'll be able to be able to get to one and a half million ARR in 18 months.

If we were to spend more money, that number would be higher. If we were able to spend an additional $400,000, on, on paid channels, assuming that our CAC only increases around 10% more given that, you know, we're mainly going to be putting into AdWords. And obviously, the more you put through that on, you know, the number of keywords that are available, that's going to bid it up a little bit, we think we'd be able to get to more like 1.9 million ARR. But the point is, is that you

actually understand the questions asked and flip the switch on the question that the investors are asking. And ultimately, you want to get to a point that if an investor asks you a financial question, you'd say, that's not the right way of thinking about our business. Here's how we think about that. If they're not asking for the right metrics, so if you really understand your numbers and what your metrics are, and you get asked that question by investors, you don't need the financial model in front of you."

In summary, startups overestimate what can be achieved in the short term and underestimate what can be done in the long term. So instead, it's better to focus on the business drivers, which will generate revenue and costs.

With respect to the addressable market, it is good to look at ballpark figures. As Alex puts it:

What matters more is the thought that goes into things and what the actual specific numbers are. And be genuinely looking for order of magnitude. So whether or not it's 617 million or 700 million. That'd be quibbling over a 30 million difference. Is that number large enough? So if you say you can only invest in a market, which is a billion dollars or more, then it doesn't matter if it's 500 million or 999 million, it's still not what you're looking for. So who cares? So long as the market is large enough?

That's literally all you're asking for. So if your triage pitch decks look at the market sizing slide. Oh, they think the market's $40 million doesn't work for my business model. DELETE. If you see that the market is $7 billion might quickly see something's cheaper or is that reasonable? So that's fine, whatever? Okay, probably fundable? Let's have a phone call. When you're digging into things in a little bit more detail, then again, what you're actually looking for is the logic that goes into it.

The most superficial 1 founder might just write like food is a $1 trillion industry, just because they actually don't really understand the industry but they saw on TechCrunch someone raised a 40 million Series A so they want to copycat the business, but they actually don't know anything about what it is they're doing. So they read that investors want to have a really big number. So they write some stupid headline number on their pitch deck, the market size and that's it. But when you ask them questions, why is it a trillion dollars? They don't actually know because they didn't spend any time thinking about it.

Investors want to know whether founders are ambitious enough. Are they logical? Do you know that going from 3 million to 90 million in a year is ridiculous? You can go 3, 9, 27, 54. Yeah, that makes sense. We have the rule of triple, triple, double, double, double, whatever, and like rule of 40% and all these little things which you can apply these heuristics to your numbers. But it's like the question is actually, do you know what you're doing?"

Non-disclosure agreements

When screening companies for angel investing, you may come across startup founders who are unwilling to show you their business plan or pitch deck unless you sign a non-disclosure agreement (NDA). The purpose of this agreement is to protect the startup company from competitors or other companies stealing their ideas.

While it is a relatively safe document to sign, and there should be no issues doing so, some angels are skeptical about signing an NDA to see the pitch deck of a startup. To be honest, we have come across few founders who ask for an NDA prior to releasing the pitch deck, as an idea in itself is rarely valuable at all without a team and execution capabilities.

In any case, there are other ways for founders to protect their ideas, so non-disclosure may be a warning sign. Unless there is a valid reason to sign one, you should be aware that an NDA will limit your ability to talk about the company with anyone, including your fellow investor syndicates or your own network.

The only exception is when the startup is a deep technology company, such as a medical device or a specific software code. There is a good reason to protect this type of company and its intellectual property from competitors. However, they are very rare and usually require specialized knowledge to evaluate properly. Moreover, the stage at which we would agree to an NDA would be past the pitch deck and the first set of meetings, and more when performing due diligence on financial models or on the product itself or demos. In these cases, we find it acceptable and low risk, so don't shy away if an NDA is required.

SECTION FIVE
Closing the deal

Now that you have found the ideal startup and have gone through successful due diligence, it is time to consider the technical details of the investment you are about to close.

Technical details will vary in different regions and countries, so it is vital that you research the tax advantages and the required formalities where you will be placing your investments. If you choose to "go global", the best way may be to follow specific angels in those regions, as they will be able to extract the value from the different investment mechanisms.

In this section, we will therefore list some of the most common terms, investment vehicles and documents that are "standard" across the startup world, as well as mentioning some of the particular instruments and tax savings in the US and UK that we have come across.

We highly recommend that you research all government and non-government incentives for investing in startups that can be found in your region since these could be incredibly valuable at the time of managing your risk.

Investment process

In our view, finding the right startups and deciding to invest is by far the most challenging part of being an angel investor. Once you have crossed that hurdle, what follows is a fairly simple process to invest your money and start helping the startup. It may seem a bit overwhelming the first couple of times you do it, but it becomes repetitive once you have mastered the steps. Below is an outline of that process after you have made up your mind.

Needless to say, processes will be slightly different in most places, but the general outline should be fairly similar. If the startup is raising very little money and you can cover the funding on your own, then the whole process will be much simpler as some of the steps will not be required.

a. Term sheet

Shortly before (or after) you decide that the founders and the startup are worth investing your time and money on, you will be given the standard terms and conditions by which the founders are raising money. A simple document known as a "term sheet" will summarize most of the terms of the deal. Here is where you will discuss the deal structure, the valuation, and other technical details. You aim to achieve a mutually acceptable deal by which you and the founders are happy today and in the future. We will discuss this later in this section.

b. Closing the round

The process doesn't end when you decide to invest in the startup. Unless the amount you are investing is enough for the startup to close the round, the startup will still be looking for other investors to complete the amount they are raising. It may be a good exercise to check what the general investor sentiment is toward the startup, as you will see how easy (or hard) it is for the founders to find all the money they need. Other investors will have other requirements on the deal, so the terms will likely end up being those that the lead investor requests.

c. **Legal documentation**
Although the term sheet contains the general structure and overview of the deal, the legal documentation will be drawn and written by lawyers. Typically, the startup will be paying for the legal drafting of documents, but there are exceptions. There shouldn't be much of a delay here since most of the documents are standard, and the commercial terms have already been discussed. However, the legal documentation usually defines a lot of the terms that will guide the relationship between the shareholders and that cannot be left to interpretation.

d. **Due diligence and anti-money laundering checks**
Bear in mind that, depending on the place of incorporation of the company, there may be due diligence on every investor. This may be required for anti-money laundering regulations or simply because the company wants to know more about every investor in order to avoid bad publicity. This will usually be performed after all terms have been set.

e. **Closing package and date**
Once all the documentation is ready and the closing date fixed, the startup will send the closing package to potential or interested investors. This will contain the documentation for them to sign, as well as the ways in which they can transfer the funds. This will end up with you being a shareholder of the company and opening the door to help them out as a new angel. From this point onwards, you have a great incentive to share your networks and help the startup in any way you can, especially so they can reach the next funding

round. If you have reached this stage, then congratulations! You can officially call yourself an angel investor.

The Term Sheet – evaluating the deal

The first and most important document in our view that you will be discussing with the founders is the so-called "term sheet".

A term sheet is a bullet-point document outlining the material terms and conditions of a potential deal, as the legal and binding documentation will be drafted later, based on the commercial terms agreed. After a term sheet has been agreed or "executed", both parties will have all they need to move on and let the lawyers do their work (mainly, draft the Shareholders Agreement and the Articles of Association if they are not already drawn up, as well as the subscription agreement).

There are plenty of sample term sheets online as well as in Angel Investor School All Access Pass section at Angel Investor School. Below we have added Y Combinator's sample TS, which is simple and includes most of the terms and issues you will probably be discussing when looking to invest as an angel. Different regions will have different specificities, but in general terms, these are the main points you need to be familiar with.

TERM SHEET

Company:	[_____], a Delaware corporation.
Securities:	Series A Preferred Stock of the Company ("**Series A**")
Investment Amounts:	$[__] million from [_____] ("**Lead Investor**") $[__] million from other investors Convertible notes and safes ("**Convertibles**") convert on their terms into shadow series of preferred stock (together with the Series A, the "**Preferred Stock**").
Valuation:	$[__] million **post-money** valuation, including an available option pool equal to [__]% of the post-Closing fully-diluted capitalization.
Liquidation Preference:	1x non-participating preference. A sale of all or substantially all of the Company's assets, or a merger (collectively, a "**Company Sale**"), will be treated as a liquidation.
Dividents:	6% noncumulative, payable if and when declared by the Board of Directors.
Conversion to Common Stock:	At holder's opinion and automatically on (i) IPO or (ii) approval of a majority of Preferred Stock (on an as-converted bias) (the "**Preferred Majority**"). Conversion ratio initially 1-to-1, subject to standard adjustments.
Voting Rights:	Approval of the Preferred Majority required to (i) change rights, preferences or privileges of the Preferred Stock; (ii) change the authorized number of shares; (iii) create securities senior or pari passu to the existing Preferred Stock; (iv) redeem or repurchase any shares (except for purchases at cost upon termination of services or exercises of contractual rights of first refusal); (v) declare or pay any dividend; (vi) change the authorized number of directors; or (vii) liquidate or dissolve, including a Company Sale. Otherwise votes with Common Stock on an asconverted basis.

Drag-Along:	Founders, investors and 1% stockholders required to vote for a Company Sale approved by (i) the Board, (ii) the Preferred Majority and (iii) a majority of Common Stock [(excluding shares of Common Stock issuable or issued upon conversion of the Preferred Stock)] (the "**Common Majority**"), subject to standard exceptions.
Other Rights & Matters:	The Preferred Stock will have standard broad-based average anti-dilution rights, pro rata rights and information rights. Company counsel drafts documents. Company pays Lead Investor's legal fees, capped at $30,000.
Board:	[Lead Investor designates 1 director. Common Majority designates 2 directors.]
Founder and Employee Vesting:	Founders: [_____]. Employees: 4-year monthly vesting with 1-year cliff.
No Shop:	For 30 days, the Company will not solicit, encourage or accept any offers for the acquisition of Company capital stock (other than equity compensation for service providers), or of all or any substantial portion of Company assets.

It is important to know what is standard in terms of negotiating the terms in this agreement. Our ambassador Anthony Rose mentions how he tackles the negotiating process:

The company shareholders agreements and articles are 30 pages of fairly dense legals. There are all sorts of little things about an IPO and stuff like that. But actually, they're probably five key things.

***So thing number one**, would obviously be the valuation and the amount that the company is raising. If the valuation is too high, this means the company, if it can't get the traction, it's* promising, will probably need a down round later. Which will dilute the founders and the investors and the investors want to protect against it. So if an investor thinks that the valuation is too high, they might respond by asking for shares with anti-dilution properties. Which is kind of telling the founder, so if your investor is asking for preferred shares with anti-dilution, it might be consciously or subconsciously your investor going: "I will buy into your crazy valuation sure, but if it doesn't live up to it on the next round, you're going to top up my shares as if your valuation would have been lower". So valuation is number one.

Number two is founder share vesting. As the investor, you're investing at my crazy 2 million valuation. And the founders, let's say own 70% of the shares. So on paper, between them, they're millionaires because of my investment. What I don't want is them selling out of the company and disappearing some weeks later with their gains while I'm left with nothing.

I want to make sure that they need my permission, at least in the short term if they sell their shares. And number two, if they leave, they get fired, they get bored, they join Google whatever, they have to give back some of their shares so that it goes to the next person. Shares vesting is super important.

Number three is a board seat. What you want as an investor, if you don't have any protections, you're at the mercy of the company doing a range of things. They might issue more shares that dilute you. The founders might want to sell their shares or sell the company, maybe they want to pivot into some completely different space that you didn't want to be involved in at all.

How do you make sure that a combination of the company can run its business on its own without needing interventions *from the investors all the time? But major things need some investor inputs, and that is achieved number one, with the investors potentially having a board seat. So that means the investors collectively, generally appoint a person as the Investor Director, and they sit on the company's board, and they represent certain things that need the consent of the investors. The alternative or an additional way is what's called investor consent. Certain things need the consent of generally the majority set by the number of shares held; 50% of the investors, the company needs their agreement to do some things. Now this is really probably the most interesting thing for both the investors and the founder. For the founders, you need to be able to run your business on a daily basis without needing investor consent.*

So if I want to hire a new developer, I should not need to go to my investors and ask their consent. But if I want to sell a company, change my business completely, maybe I've raised 200,000 pounds, and I now want to hire a new marketing guy, my cousin, for 200,000 pounds. I'm going to run out of money, this is clearly a stupid thing to do. So investor consents, or board approval, which has an investor on the board, would be needed. I think this is probably the key thing, which is, to find the right checks and balances so that the founders can run the business on a daily basis without really asking the investors, but the investors have assurance that big things need their approval.

One of the fascinating ways and I love the way SeedLegals can help is we can show with data, how these approvals and mechanisms change with different stages of the company. So if you're raising 100,000 pounds, and you've got an idea, there's no team, there's no revenue, for sure, you don't want investor consent and investor directors because you don't know what your budget is. You have to change on a weekly basis what you're doing to find product market fit. Having those consent rights would be wrong at a super early stage.

On the other hand, if you're raising a few million pounds, for sure your investors are going to insist on that and there's no point having a big fight because it always is the case. So the investor consents, the investor director position would be probably thing number three. What other things might there be?

Number four is the share classes that the investors get. This is one of the fantastic things about SEIS and EIS (UK government backed investment scheme) for a founder. Because in order for an investor to get SEIS, EIS tax benefits, they have to take what's called the ordinary risks of an investor. Which means you can't promise to buy their shares back again, you can't promise to top them up. So they can't get many of the things that VCs want that disadvantage the founders. VCs will want preference shares that give them their money back first on a sale of the company.

They might want anti-dilution. They might want a warrant or something in a future round. You can't give that to an investor if they want SEIS or EIS. So, the next important thing is what preference rights or anti-dilutions should you give to an investor. There again, we can guide companies. The good news is with SEIS and EIS, it will force the investors to have ordinary shares so this is less of an issue if you have a UK angel investor. But if you have a fund or a foreign investor, they may ask for those preference shares.

Number five is the warranties. This is something that most people don't know. And they come across it for the first time. They go, what is this about? When an investor invests in your company, they're doing it based on some promises you've made. You've told them, I've got no debt, we own all the shares, there's no strange holding company. I haven't promised money to a friend. This is the business. We're not being sued by anybody and so on. But what if you just were laxed in making these promises? Or what if you lied? The investor is going to want their money back. If they discover they've invested in a business, and actually it's not at all what you've promised, they're going to want their money back.

The way they might discover this is at the time of your next tax return, when a whole load of financials may be disclosed. So that's called the disclosure and the warranties. It's a funny game where you tell you investor, I promise you the following 87 things are true but if they're not true, this is where you disclose them. So you might say, the company owes no money to anybody. The company owes no taxes. But then you might go, actually where it says that there's no money, actually, it owes me 12,000 pounds, I've put in a loan. Then the investor reads through all of these and goes oh, yeah, that's fine. That's fine. I agree to that.

By seeing the list of disclosures, if the investor still wishes to go ahead and invest, then they can't sue the company or founder for that afterwards. So this warranty and disclosure system is something that is a completely new concept to most founders, and in fact, often to investors. But it's a key part of funding rounds, particularly when we're raising some hundreds of thousands of pounds later. What we also try and do on SeedLegals is these are quite custom, there might be any number of disclosures. So we tried to create a standardised framework, and a standardised set of objective things.

Sometimes American investors want crazy warranties, like, you warrant that the company will be earning this revenue in the future. I can't do that, I have no idea stuff doesn't work that way in startup land. We don't have any of those. We only have things that you'd either have been really sloppy or lying if they weren't true. So the company owns its assets, the company has these shares, these are the current shareholders. These are things you can verify and we try to make those super easy to complete.

The other part of this is if you have misled the investor, then they might want their money back so they can claim against the company but they can usually also claim against the founder. The problem is the company might be bankrupt, so they want to claim against the founder. But you don't want to have raised a million pounds and now be personally liable for a million pounds. That's very bad. So on SeedLegals, we let you limit the founders personal liability, and we suggest about 10% of the amount raised, split between the founders. So, if you're raising a million pounds, and the two founders, we might say 50,000 pounds per founder, typically more like five to 20,000 pounds per founder. It's the sort of thing that the investors know that you're taking seriously.

But it shouldn't be the point that will drive you out of your house. 'Honey, things went wrong for you need to move to a caravan, sorry about that.' You don't want that. It's probably one of the key personal protections that we ensure. But the 90% use case is you have another funding round in the next 12 months, that overwrites all of this anyway. You needed to have made sure it was good law to get you to the next place that you didn't have to obsess about too many future things. Because actually, there's a high likelihood it's just going to be overwritten in your next round anyway."

Contents of the term sheet

a. The offering

This section of the document will include formal details such as:

- ✓ Name of the company or issuer of the shares (holding company)
- ✓ Place of incorporation

This is very important as the laws and regulations of the place of incorporation will drive the legal protections and terms, regardless of the place (or places) of operation of the company.

- ✓ Type of shares being issued (typically ordinary or preferred)
  - **Ordinary shares:** typically reserved for founders, employees, and advisors. Shareholders holding ordinary shares will not have any preference in the case of sale or liquidation of a company. This means they will be the last to get paid after all preferred shareholders have been paid.
  - **Preferred shares:** These are the most commonly used shares in the startup and VC world. They have a preference (or seniority) over ordinary shares and will be paid before ordinary in case of a sale or liquidation of the company. Other than liquidation preference, preferred shares usually contain anti-dilution provisions (more on preference below).
- ✓ Amount of the offering (or total size of the round)
- ✓ Price per share (or calculating mechanism)
- ✓ Name of the investor
- ✓ Closing date
- ✓ Valuation

The price is the percent of ownership given to the investor, or post-money valuation. The pre-money valuation is the startup's value today, while the post-money is the pre-money plus any investments made in the particular round. We believe that for startups, no formula will give you a precise valuation. It is useful to get the market to set the valuation or a lead investor. You can also look at comparable companies that have recently raised. The valuation needs to be something that the founders are comfortable with, which will allow them to raise enough funds and avoid too much dilution, and that will be attractive for enough investors. Let's have a look at the next important point, which is share vesting.

When looking at valuation, it is important to differentiate between pre-money and post-money valuation. In the words of Alejandro Cremades:

 Pre-money is basically the valuation that you agree with the lead investor. And basically, let's say if you're doing a pre-money of $20 million and you're raising, let's say $5 million, the pre-money is $20 million and the post-money is going to be $25 million. Because here's the $20 million from the pre-money plus the injection of new capital coming in, the $5 million. So the post-money is 25. Pre-money is before the investment round closes and a post-money is once the round has closed, and once all of that pre-money and all the money taken in, what all that amounts to."

b. General terms of the issuance

This section becomes slightly more complex as there are terms that may not be familiar to new angels, but that should be mastered before discussing your first investment. We will define and quickly describe the most important terms you will find in a term sheet.

Shares preference and liquidation rights

As an angel investor, you will likely be investing at the very beginning of the fundraising process of a startup. This means that before you, probably only founders (and employees) are the only shareholders. And given they will have been issued with ordinary shares, you will be the only one with preferred shares. Should there be an exit sale, liquidation, or winding up of the company, you will receive whatever is left (assuming there is something left to sell).

As the funding series move on, it is customary that the last investors to come in will be paid first. Also known as LIFO (Last In, First Out), this is a mechanism by which VCs and investors are compensated for the risk they are assuming given higher valuations (and larger check sizes).

Within the preference level, shareholders will receive shares proportional to the amount of equity that they own. For example, Series A investors must be fully paid up before Seed investors are paid. If there is just enough to pay 50% of Seed investments, all Seed investors will receive half of what they invested.

Moreover, investors may be able to negotiate that they need to receive a certain number of times their investment before the next investors receive anything. The negotiating powers of VCs writing large checks may allow them to request this from the startup. Any of these provisions that you manage to negotiate as an angel will be included in the term sheet.

Share counts

Another technical point, which may appear in the term sheet is the share counts. These are important as they are the denominator in the cap table, and therefore will allow you to understand your percentage in the company. As the startups grow, cap tables become increasingly complex, and legal counsel becomes a necessity. However, as an angel investor, investing in the early stages of a company, you don't need to worry much. Think that if the company is growing and becoming super complex, all this means is that your investment is growing exponentially.

That being said, the main definitions that you may find in a term sheet that you need to understand at this stage are:

Authorized Shares – Authorized shares refer to the number of shares authorized for current and future issuance.

Outstanding Shares – This is the total number of shares issued.

Fully Diluted Shares – This is a calculation that will include all the outstanding shares, options, restricted stock, warrants, employee share option plans, and the remainder of the option pool. This number will be theoretical and will help you understand your percentage holding, should all shares be issued and options exercised.

Conversion

Conversion is also important as many times, you will be investing in convertible notes that "convert" into shares or stock as per pre-defined rates, valuations, and conditions. We will discuss what convertible notes are below.

Preferred stock is more valuable than common stock as it grants certain rights. One of which is a conversion right.

There are several types of conversion, but the most common are mandatory and optional. Mandatory conversion will oblige the holder to convert at a specific value when specific conditions are met. Optional conversion gives you the option to convert, usually from preferred to common stock at a higher multiple (as you will be losing any preference rights in case of liquidation).

Dividends

It is also likely, especially if you invest via convertible notes, that these have an interest or dividend. There are many ways in which a startup can sweeten the deal, especially if the investors are coming in at the early stages without a priced valuation. If the priced valuation happens 12 to 18 months away, an interest or dividend may be included in the deal.

Even if the investor is acquiring shares in a priced round, there may also be a dividend (similar to listed equity). However, in the case of startups, this dividend is not guaranteed and not paid regularly. There may also be provisions by which the dividend is accumulated in the form of preference shares and paid upon IPO or a different liquidity event.

Share selling and buying rights

One of the most important aspects of the term sheet and the negotiating process is selling and buying rights. There will be instances where new investors want to clear the cap table (or get rid of small investors) or when you believe that the startup is going well and therefore you want to keep investing in order to keep your percentage. You, therefore, need to know what you can negotiate and ask the company.

Pre-emption rights

Pre-emption rights give investors the right to purchase more shares to keep their level of investment in the company in subsequent rounds (at the new valuation). There is no obligation, and angel investors rarely make follow-on investments. However, it is usually recommended that you keep some money aside for those special cases in which you love a company that is growing steadily and has massive potential to scale. Your rights to buy more shares will be proportional or pro-rata to your holdings.

These are also a type of anti-dilution rights, and you may find language in the term sheet that will not allow you to sell these rights to third parties (therefore, you, and only you, can purchase more shares). These provisions will be included since the founders will always want to control who becomes a shareholder in their company.

Right of first refusal (ROFR)

Pre-emptive rights and pro-rata rights protect the investor in the sale of new shares or new funding rounds. As an angel investor, you can also request protection in a secondary offering or sale of existing shares. Known as ROFR (right of first refusal), this clause will allow existing shareholders to buy shares from any selling shareholder before new investors. This will be at the same conditions agreed with third parties. It is likely that the company will also have the option to buy the stock from the selling shareholder.

Drag along, Tag along

Next, we have **"drag-along"** rights. If there is a sale of the startup as a whole, the buying investor may want to acquire all shares. This becomes a problem when there are small investors included who may want to block the sale. Although any majority shareholder can sell their shares, they cannot force smaller shareholders to do the same unless the documentation has foreseen this circumstance. This is where "drag-along" provisions and rights come in. This is not a right for you as an angel but an obligation to sell if certain conditions are met. It can also be considered good for minority shareholders as they will receive the same deal conditions in the sale as the majority ones.

On the other side, **"tag-along"** or co-sale rights are usually in place to protect minority shareholders. They give shareholders the rights (but not the obligation) to sell or buy at the same conditions as the majority shareholders. So if there is any movement or if the big guys find great deals, smaller shareholders can "tag-along" and get the same treatment.

The following is a sample ROFR and tag along or co-sale clause:

> *The Investors shall have a pro-rata right, but not an obligation, based on their ownership of Ordinary Shares, to participate on identical terms in transfers of any shares of the Company, and a right of first refusal on such transfers (subject to customary permitted transfers, including transfers by Investors to affiliated funds). Any shares not subscribed for by the Investors would then be offered to the other holders of Ordinary Shares.*
>
> *So long as any of the Preferred are outstanding, consent of the majority of the then-outstanding Preferred will be required for any action that (i) amends the Articles of the Corporation if it would adversely alter the rights, preferences, privileges or powers of Preferred; (ii) changes the number of directors from current number; or (iii) approves any merger, asset sale, liquidation or other corporate reorganization or acquisition."*

Board and voting rights

It is very important to have a board to keep good governance and accountability in place. As our ambassador Anthony Thomson points out:

> *I think that the whole purpose of the board is first to support the management through their experience and expertise. Second, is to challenge the management and to ensure that the decisions that the management are taking or proposing to take, have been well thought through and are in the best interest of the business. I'm a great believer in the boards that I've chaired in creating diversity in every respect of the word; cultural diversity, diversity by gender, and so on and so forth. In my experience over the years, it does bring in differing views. There is a criticism addressed at a lot of boards, which is they are, male, pale and stale. They're full of middle aged, old white blokes like me and I think there's a lot of truth in that.*

Whereas, the better boards are those that are encouraging and engendering diversity because the audiences, our customers are diverse. We need to make sure that we understand them and we reflect them in the composition of our boards."

For angel investors, having board seats is not the norm but rather the exception. In some cases, it is likely that the startup wants to have an angel investor on its board. This gives higher credibility and visibility to the startup. This is the example of Dan Scheinman on Zoom's board.

But these are the exceptions. Board seats are usually reserved either for VCs or lead investors. In any case, it is good to know what the boards usually decide on, and if you are investing a significant amount of money in the particular round, it is quite likely that you will want some sort of oversight in the operations of the startup.

The composition and decision power of the board will be drawn by external counsel in the articles of association and in the shareholders agreement, but some key decisions to be taken by the board (or by investors) can also be included in the term sheet (though less likely). A simplified clause in the term sheet could look like this:

Certain important actions of the Company shall require the consent of the [Lead investor/board/majority], to include amongst others, actions to: (i) alter the rights of the Ordinary Shares (ii) allot any new shares beyond those anticipated by this investment (iii) create any new class or series senior to the Ordinary Shares (iv) increase the number of shares reserved for issuance to employees and consultants, whether under the ESOP or otherwise (v) redeem or the selling of any shares (vi) pay or declare dividends or distributions to shareholders (vii) change the number of board members (viii) take any action which results in a Change of Control (ix) amend the constitutional documents including the by-laws or shareholders

agreements (x) effect any material change to the nature of the business plan (xi) subscribe or otherwise acquire, or dispose of any shares in the capital of any other company."

The rules on voting will be clearly set in the legal documentation, and standard templates are often used. The risk at the angel level will not be on these decisions, so this is not something to worry about at this stage.

However, for information purposes, there can be several ways to approve or reject motions. For example, a preferred majority may be required for certain actions mentioned in the term sheet. In that case, preferred shareholders (so not the founders or employees) have veto power on certain topics.

On the other hand, if a "common" majority is stipulated, it will be the common shareholders who decide on those issues together with the preferred shareholders (unless they don't have common voting rights).

Make sure you understand that the founders will be running the company and not the investors or the board. Excessive interference from the board or individual investors can cripple the company, so there should be a balance in decision-making, and only key issues should be decided by the board.

Information rights

Finally, shareholders and investors have a right to know periodically what is happening with the company. These can be monthly, quarterly, or at the discretion of the founders, but it is always advisable that there is a set deadline for the company to tell you how the business is going. This gives you the potential to help or offer help in challenging times, as well as to get joy when things are going well.

It's good to ask founders for weekly/fortnightly / monthly updates, which could be in the form of a group message to all investors, which could be useful to understand how angels can help at different intervals of time. This also demonstrates loyalty once the highly craved money has been secured.

Capitalization table

As an early-stage investor, your objective is to get into the capitalization table (or cap table in short) of the startup by offering your funds, as well as those extra bits such as your time and contacts.

The cap table shows all the shareholders, how many shares there are, how much has been paid for them, and what type they are. There are five kinds of people on a cap table: founders, employees, advisors, angels, and VCs. Founders start with 100% of the company. Employees get shares generally out of an option pool. This means that if they stay with the company for a set amount of time, they will have an option to buy shares at a much lower strike price based on the company valuation at the time of issuing the options. It helps employees keep motivated as they become owners of the company. Options are generally vested so that, for example, if they become callable after four years of staying in the company, a person could get 50% of the shares if they decided to leave after just two years of work. Advisors are people that will advise companies and lend their name for reputational reasons in exchange for some equity. VCs are firms that invest in early-stage and help them transition into scale-ups.

In a cap table, you would also have a syndicate of angels. We will talk about this in a further section.

Investment structures

As an angel, you should review all deal structures and determine which ones are likely to fit into your angel profile. You may find that certain types of investment opportunities are more likely to be a good fit for your angel profile, while other deal structures are not as well suited to you.

There are multiple different structures that angels investors can use to invest in startups:

Convertible note

Convertible debt is a loan that an investor makes to a company using a convertible note, a financing instrument. This is the typical way that angels invest in startups. A convertible note gives investors the option at some point after a set time in the future to "convert" the notes into equity. These notes will have a maturity date (when the principal and interest need to be repaid) and convert into equity when a company does an equity fundraising round. They come with a discount if the startup is acquired or goes public.

The most common structure is when the angel gets a 20% discount on the note if the company does either of those things.

When the notes are interest-bearing, they have some cap on how much interest can accumulate each month. In addition, they are often given a deadline by which to convert them into equity. If this deadline is not met, then the option to convert goes away.

This approach is appealing to angels because it gives them better protection than just being an investor with nothing more than a share of common stock in exchange for their money. The downside is that these notes generally come with caps on the amount of money that can be raised, and they also expect you to have your money back within a certain time frame.

Our ambassador Alejandro Cremades points out the main bits to consider about convertible notes:

 So on convertible notes, basically, there's four different things that a founder and that investor need to look at. It is basically the interest that you're giving away to investors for the money that they're giving you. Right now what I'm seeing is about 5%

to 8% interest. Then there is the discount that you're going to be giving on the valuation of that company when they get to the next qualified financing round, which is going to happen in the Series A. And that's where institutional investors come in. The discount, typically what I'm seeing right now is between 15% to 20%, something along those lines, and that's on the valuation. So for example, if it's, let's say, a 20% discount that you're getting for a convertible note, and then a Series A happens, and there's a $20 million pre-money valuation, and you're kicking in at $18 million pre rather than $20 million pre.

And then you have the valuation cap. So some of those notes are capped or not capped. And what the cap means is that indirectly, you're establishing a valuation for the round. And basically, for example, if we take the $20 million pre-money example, that means that if you give it a valuation cap of let's say, $5 million, or let's say $10 million. If it's a $10 million valuation cap you're giving on the note, that means that even if you've gone to $20 million pre, those investors are still coming in at $10 million. Now, here's the tricky part. Because if you bought a valuation cap of $10 million, but the valuation is not $20 million, but actually is under $10 million, then basically the discount of 20% would kick in that we were discussing earlier.

Either on going above or going below, you're still going to be capturing the value of it as an investor, if there is a cap. You're going have the maturity date on convertible notes. The maturity date means when the debt needs to be either rebated, or when that debt is converted into equity. Typically, what happens is that the people that are investing in convertible notes are well aligned with the founder. And basically what happens is that those notes convert into equity, and they continue to push forward, as equity holders, once the next institutional round happens. The equity round basically is very straightforward, putting a valuation of the business. Basically you're going to *have the subscription agreement on the other documents that are going to be determining what's going to happen around the corporate structure of their business."*

Common stock

The next most common way that angels invest is by exchanging money for a share of the company's common stock. This is one of the least flexible structures, but it does mean that you can acquire a much larger stake in the company as an angel since there are no limits on how much you can put into it.

In addition, you are not limited to just one round of investment. You can invest a large amount of money in one round, then come back later and invest again. Startup companies generally welcome follow-on investments by angels, and you can discuss this at the time of investing and set some clauses that can be applied in future funding rounds.

This approach is appealing to founders because it does not put them at risk for any debt repayment like the convertible note structure does. It also means that angels can invest a lot more money into the startup at one time. However, this structure does mean that they stand to lose all their investment if the company goes under, so they need to be very comfortable with the team and business model if they choose this route.

Preferred stock

Angel investors sometimes choose to invest in exchange for preferred stock rather than common stock (if they are allowed to). This stock type comes with specific rights, privileges, and preferences when compared with common stock.

Most importantly, "preferred" stock means that you get paid before anyone else when it comes time for a liquidation event. This is desirable since you will get your money back before the common stockholders. The terms are usually that the preferred stock gets paid out first, then common stockholders get whatever is left over.

Preferred stock can usually be converted into common stock at a liquidity moment, such as an IPO or an acquisition.

It's good to dig into the experience of Alejandro Cremades:

 So, the difference is really like what is your order in the line really when there is a liquidity event. Meaning like when the company gets acquired or does an IPO and so forth. It is like, who is first in line to really cash out. Basically the preferred stock is what gives the preferential right or treatment to those investors that are coming in later. So, the more rounds that you do, the bigger the incentives are on those preferred stocks that they receive because the equation is that last money in, is first money out. It is always like that.

So, for example, as you were saying the difference between common and preferred, typically common is what founders, directors, advisors, and employees are going to be receiving. And the preferred is what investors are going to be receiving. When you do a good acquisition, maybe you've raised, just to put a number, like $20 million, and you've raised 20 million at maybe a $60 or $70 million valuation. If you're getting your company acquired by anything over that or it depends on the liquidation events there, and the 1x, 2x or whatever they put in there. But if it's an up-round or a valuation on the acquisition, it's okay. The problem really becomes when, for example, if you raised a $70 million valuation, and the company is acquired for anything under $70 million, then it becomes tricky. It becomes tricky because maybe as a common stockholder, there's not enough money to cover for the preferred stock in order to only pay out the common stockholders. So that's when it really becomes problematic.

> And where you've seen cases like, for example, like the founders of FanDuel, selling the business for $450 million, but then giving all the preferred stock that was in front of them, they ended up with zero. Those are the nightmares that you would see. It's very unfortunate, but not all the time. Even though they are saying great exits, the founder, for the most part, doesn't make money because of those different layers of preferential treatment that other investors get."

Debt

It may not always be an option for you to invest in a startup, and sometimes the best option is to provide the company with debt financing.

Debt comes with a fixed interest rate, which gives the startup more predictable cash flow. It also gives you a higher risk profile because you will get paid back before any equity investors do if there is ever a liquidation event. You will get your money back first, and then others can divide up what's left after that. The downside of debt is that you won't achieve an exponential return on your investment, as the interest rate that you agree to receive is fixed.

Typical investment vehicles

Although there are tons of different ways for you to subscribe shares of a startup (starting with simply giving money to a friend for them to invest and agreeing verbally what your percentage holding will be), over the past few years, there are several websites, platforms and documentation sets that have made things easy for both investors and founders when it comes to fundraising.

There are many different tax schemes and documentation types, as these vary per region and depend on the regulation of individual countries. We strongly recommend that you research the investment vehicles and tax schemes available in your country. Here are some examples:

SAFE

One such documentation set is called SAFE (simple agreement for future equity), which is one of the most common types of documentation used for early-stage investments in the US and across the world. SAFE is similar to convertible debt but without interest, maturity, and repayment requirements.

SAFE was introduced by one of the largest accelerators in the world, called Y Combinator. In 2013 YC designed a set of documentation, which would be later used by almost all the startups that came from their accelerator and later by many more startups across the world. Many view SAFE as the best main instrument for early-stage fundraising.

In the early days, the SAFE was a "pre-money" safe, a simple and fast way to get that first money into the company, and the concept was that holders of SAFEs were merely early investors in that future priced round. Investors at that stage were not given equity but something similar to a convertible note, which promised equity based on a set of conditions but not a certain valuation. This meant that investors would get the valuation set at a later date with a discount. It avoided the discussions between investors and the startup regarding the accurate valuation, something that in early-stage ventures is more of an art than math.

As early-stage fundraising developed, SAFE was adjourned to catch-up with the developing markets and fundraising mechanisms. In this sense, SAFE moved from pre-money to post-money SAFE. According to YC:

By "post-money," we mean that safe holder ownership is measured after (post) all the safe money is accounted for - which is its own round now - but still before (pre) the new money in the priced round that converts and dilutes the safes (usually the Series A, but sometimes Series Seed). The post-money safe has what we think is a huge advantage for both founders and investors - the ability to calculate immediately and precisely how much ownership of the company has been sold. It's critically important for founders to understand how much dilution is caused by each safe they sell, just as it is fair for investors to know how much ownership of the company they have purchased.

The SAFE has two fundamental features that are critically important for startups:

- ✓ It allows for high-resolution fundraising. Startups can close with an investor as soon as both parties are ready to sign and the investor is ready to wire money instead of trying to coordinate a single close with all investors simultaneously. In fact, high-resolution fundraising may be much easier now that both founders and investors have more certainty and transparency into what each side is giving and getting.

- ✓ As a flexible, one-document security without numerous terms to negotiate, SAFEs save startups and investors money in legal fees and reduce the time spent negotiating the terms of the investment. Startups and investors will usually only have to negotiate one item: the valuation cap. Because a SAFE has no expiration or maturity date, there should be no time or money spent dealing with extending maturity dates, revising interest rates, or the like.

SAFE notes will take into account investor and founder situations and create a document that suits many situations and intends to be balanced. It is a simple and comprehensive document and can be very useful for starting negotiations (and/or finishing them).

SAFE notes are now also useful in the UK (using the SeedFAST agreement) and in many other parts of the world, thus becoming more popular.

UK Seed Enterprise Investment Scheme (SEIS) and Enterprise Investment Scheme (EIS)

Other interesting schemes are the UK's SEIS and EIS schemes, both of which provide excellent risk-mitigating mechanisms for those liable for taxes in the UK.

Born in 2012, Seed Enterprise Investment Scheme (SEIS) is an initiative that the UK government set up to incentivize investment in small and seed-stage startups. In a nutshell, a company can raise up to £150,000, and those investing receive tax relief. The idea behind the government's initiative is to mitigate private investors' risks in startups with a view to helping grow the sector and entrepreneurship as a whole.

SEIS has advantages for both companies and investors. For companies, the main advantage is that startups can raise up to £150,000 under the scheme. Companies can use these funds to grow or repay loans for trade, as long as the loans are not connected to the investor entering the scheme and need to be used within two years of the companies' start date. Investment must represent a risk for the investors (so it cannot be collateralized or protected).

Regarding investors, main advantages lie in the tax deductions that can be made:

i. Up to 50% income tax relief

ii. Capital Gains Tax (CGT) relief of 50% on other non-SEIS investments provided the gains are reinvested into SEIS

iii. If the shares in the SEIS company are held for three years or more, there is no CGT payable on the sale (in case there are gains)

iv. If the company goes bust, the investor can claim part of the investment back, depending on their individual tax circumstances.

v. No inheritance tax

vi. Tax relief can be carried back to the previous tax year.

In terms of conditions to access the scheme, investors must be UK taxpayers, can't be employees or paid directors of the company they are investing in, and can't invest more than £100,000 in SEIS each year. The government also excludes family members (spouses, civil partners, parents, and children) in the scheme, so be careful if a close relative is willing to invest. Finally, the investor must not hold more than 30% of the company too.

This is just a quick snapshot for UK investors. There are some intricacies in the scheme, so we recommend reading sites such as Seedlegals.com, which provide great updated sources of information and very clear guides.

An equivalent scheme with slightly different conditions is called Enterprise Investment Scheme (EIS), which will allow for smaller deductions for individual investors, but larger potential for fundraising for companies.

As mentioned before, we strongly advise you to check if there are any formalities in your region or country and any tax incentive schemes. This may simplify the process for you, as well as reduce your tax impact, or allow you to compensate for losses, thus massively reducing your risk when venturing into the world of early-stage startups.

UK Seedfast

A SeedFAST is an SEIS/EIS-friendly way for startups to raise cash ahead of a funding round. Created by SeedLegals, it offers an Advanced Subscription Agreement ("ASA").

SeedFASTs allow investors to subscribe for shares in the next funding round in exchange for their giving you money now. SeedFAST is a carefully worded, easy-to-understand document, which complies with SEIS and EIS legislation.

It's a quick and inexpensive way to raise funds from individual investors to continue growing your business without having to corral a group of investors into a funding round and having to agree to a valuation, fixed close date, and long-form legals. In summary, it is an ASA that complies with UK law.

Getting legal support as an angel investor

With a lot of legal documentation to go through, you may ask yourself whether you need to get a lawyer involved in a transaction, as this can add quite a lot of cost to an early-stage transaction. Luckily, the industry is moving toward making legal documentation into a commodity rather than a tailored document for every raise.

For example, SeedLegals in the UK market provides standard documentation for companies raising investment, incentivizing their teams with share options, doing their SEIS/EIS, and managing their cap tables. With one in six early-stage funding rounds now on SeedLegals, they have transformed how UK companies start, grow, and scale.

According to our ambassador Anthony Rose, CEO and Founder of Seedlegals, as an angel in the UK, you don't necessarily need lawyers, as long as the startups subscribe to services such as those offered by SeedLegals.

> *Firstly, if the company is on SeedLegals, we think the investors don't need a lawyer. And why is that? Well, firstly, if you imagine, what are the key risks for the investor? So the risks of course, product, team, legal, and others. I think the legal risk is*

not the greatest risk; the greatest risk is the company is going to run out of money or spend so much on legal fees that they could have hired another developer and gotten there faster. But in terms of the legal risk area, firstly, you want to make sure that the founders have got their founder agreements in place so that if things do go wrong, the company can continue and recover neatly from that. Secondly, the investor wants to see the key deal terms. In particular, most angel investors are looking for SEIS or EIS tax deductions, which has got several benefits.

You write off 50 or 35 percent by sending your investments against your tax. If the company folds or goes under, you can write off your investment. And if you keep your shares for three years, you pay no capital gains tax on an exit. So it is a fantastic win for investors, but they want to make sure that the company is going to do the things it needs to do so that they get that if the company messes up in the share allocations or forgets to do things, the investors may not get their SEIS or EIS tax deductions. And if that was a key reason to invest, you want to make sure that's the case. The next thing I think, ultimately, is you want to make sure no one's to trust that you and the founders are entering into good faith into some arrangement and there's no hidden gotchas.

Normally in the past, when someone sent me a shareholder agreement, you'd sit there with a few espressos and for hours and bits of paper, looking at definitions going in any one paragraph, someone's trying to screw me, I just need to find out where it is. The goal with SeedLegals is to actually show you. These are the key terms in plain English, you want an investor, director, seat, this investor consent, you're getting this type of shares. I can look at that and then of course, I might want to or should read the legals to double check it. But actually, I can see at a glance, what I'm getting, and hopefully, trust that the platform will have generated the legals to reflect that. So it's all about helping two parties get to a common framework and understanding and seeing what is marketed and then trusting that the documents will reflect that."

There are other sites helping investors simplify matters, such as Carta in the US. Carta is a transfer agent for private companies that enables seed-stage pre-IPO companies to manage equity electronically with the participation of their shareholders, employees, auditors, and legal counsel. It digitizes paper stock certificates along with stock options, warrants, and derivatives to create a real-time image of who owns what at a startup.

The bottom line: if it doesn't feel right, just say no

Even if you have gone through the due diligence process and decided this was a good investment, the final stages may prove you right or wrong. This is the last stage before you commit and deploy your capital, so any new information, including how the founders behave at this stage, is super important. If something does not feel right, you may need to trust your gut and pull out from the deal. Developing an investment instinct is probably the most important skill that you will need as an angel.

Although this may seem obvious, saying no to someone who has invested time in trying to sell you their startup may be quite hard. It is even harder if whoever is fundraising is a friend or a family member and after they have committed time to answer your questions, demo their product, present documentation, etc. So you need to start the process by abstracting yourself from the emotions.

As our ambassador Carlos Blanco would put it:

> *Do not invest in friends!. Don't invest in friends unless that friend is great at what he does. But at first it's hard for you to know, and if you invest in a friend, do it as a follower. And if not, think of that money as a donation. Take it from another budget, from your social side. We all have a social side. Well, maybe if you invest in friends knowing it's going to go wrong, don't even count it as an investment. Do it on your social side, because we are all NGOs at some point."*

But be sure that when you do invest, you do so with confidence and the knowledge that, even if you did the best due diligence, over 90% of technology startups fail. So rest assured that your friends will likely still be your friends even if you don't invest in them, as the odds are always against them.

Or say 'not yet'. Keep them interested if you were interested but not fully convinced at this point. Create an incentive for them to prove you wrong and build a better company. After all, they will likely be fundraising in the next 12 to 18 months anyway (unless they went bust), so your money, connections, and expertise may still be valuable to them at that time. A 'not yet' also has the advantage of not crushing the emotions of the founders. It is also useful to ask founders to get you onto their monthly updates list. They may not have one yet, but it is useful that they create one to keep investors happy and establish initial governance.

Keeping notes and memos

Finally, when you do start investing, you will find yourself making mistakes and making great investments. At the beginning, we are sorry to say that it is more likely to make mistakes than to be lucky with the startups you pick. But do not despair. This is why most of our ambassadors recommend diversifying your portfolio as one of their top recommendations. This simply follows math and the probability of startups failing vs. becoming unicorns.

However, we have learned from the best that we should keep notes and clear memos of what went wrong and what went right in each of our investments. It may seem obvious at first or with the first couple of checks. But this can get complex quickly as you start writing several checks each year. It is likely that you will forget. As our ambassador Gokul Rajaram puts it:

 With investments, it's important to at least have a good way of categorising them. The way I manage them is to simply have a large Google spreadsheet with one tab per year. I think of essentially, since I've been angel investing for now 13 years, there's 13 tabs in it. So I think of angel investments from a vintage year, which is the year I made the investment. And I'll basically go back and see every two to three months, definitely once a quarter, maybe more than once a quarter, the older vintages to see what lessons I can learn from them. And hopefully apply them together to get better.

So that's how I do it. Different people use different approaches but for me a more lightweight approach. I don't want any complex software, just a spreadsheet with tabs, one per year and I can see that in the initial years, I would do only four or five investments. Then there was a period where I was doing 30 investments a year for two or three years. There was a period now I'm doing a smaller number of larger investments, larger sized amount investments. So I can trace my evolution as an angel investor."

SECTION SIX
Portfolio Management

So now that you've written your first check, you are officially an angel investor! That doesn't mean you are a good one just yet. It really depends on what you have chosen. Early investors in Google received a 1000x return on their investment, and investors on eBay received a 1500x return. Statistically, there is a 0.00067% that the first company you chose will go all the way to becoming a unicorn, so make sure that you don't put all of your eggs into the same basket. The game has just begun, and it's time to discuss how you build a portfolio.

Asset allocation

The first thing you need to do is decide your asset allocation. This means you need to work out how much your net assets are worth, including your property, valuables, equity, businesses, and cash. Let's suppose your assets total $10 million. You may want to invest 10-15% of this into angel investing. This would mean you have $1 to $1.5 million to invest in early-stage companies.

You would need to decide then a target frame of time in which you will allocate the funds. A decent amount of time would be five years. If this is the case, you would have $200k to invest per year if you were investing $1 million over five years. At a rate of $25k per startup, you would have the capacity to onboard eight startups per year.

Of course, not all startups need to receive equal amounts of funding, though it is important to avoid concentration risk. Diversification is one of the most important aspects of angel investing, as we have seen plenty of times from Angel Investor School's ambassadors.

Start with a portfolio mindset

Nobody wants to miss out on a specific company. Let's say you were offered to invest in Uber in its early days, and you passed. You might feel that it is the one that got away. However, if you are seeing a lot of deals and have clear criteria on what to invest in, you will become successful at the angel investing game. The objective is to plan for high returns of 20x to 50x, rather than 1000x, as this is very unlikely and would require high concentration in just the winners. Remember, not every company you invest in can be a unicorn.

If you are playing the portfolio game, you can live with your decisions in a better way. See hundreds of deals, and pick the ones you like the most. To prepare you better, listen out the stories of two big angels below:

Dan Martell's experience:

> *Dude, I passed on Uber. You know why? Travis was an investor in my company Flowtown. I was in the jam pad in his condo when Uber taxi was launched. And I passed because Travis didn't even want to be CEO. He hired Ryan from Chicago off of Twitter to be the general manager. Travis just wanted the service. He didn't actually want to build the business. He thought*

it was a cool idea. He just didn't want to do it because he just sold Red Swoosh and he was kind of chilling out. So why would I invest? The person who started it isn't even interested in being the CEO and he hired this guy off of Twitter, Ryan Graves. He's an amazing dude. He actually just resigned to COO and he's worth 1.4 billion came in on 28 years old.

But what happened was the business went like this and then Travis took over. I'm very much a look at the situation. If it feels weird, I'm just going to pass. I'm okay being wrong. Because you know, it's a portfolio approach and over time, if you do it right, you'll get, in my case, $4 billion companies. An incredible return. My IRR is better than anything the stock market could ever give me. I'm still very active and planned on doing a whole lot more outside of my other stuff. So, life's good, no complaints."

A really good example that shows how portfolios are important. And also read Pejman Nozad's experience on missing out on Facebook

I had an opportunity to invest $50,000 in Facebook, Series B which was like under 100 million dollars valuation and then a company worth 60 billion dollars. It was down to the centre to actually publish it. If you Google that you can see even the email from the lawyers. Was down to the wire, it wasn't like I promised to invest but I it was the deal was contingent to lease one of our properties to them. We own some real estate properties and we tried to over negotiate that lease and that didn't happen. So, I learned that you have to see forest with the trees and don't over analyse the situation early on.

And don't negotiate for four cents extra or low. I think that was the biggest mistake I made. I lost money, I lost investments, I lost opportunity, other companies. When I look back, all of them, I really saw the founder as exceptional and I over

analyzed the market, or the competition. When you invest this early you need to believe the future through the eyes of entrepreneurs. That's something I'm going to keep reminding myself of."

So, in summary, make sure that you invest in several companies, following a portfolio strategy, and remembering that the founders are the most important asset that a company has at this stage. And prepare to lose money on even 50% of your deals. As Fabrice Grinda explains, on average, he has lost money in half his deals. So to date, he has about 600 investments and around 200 exits and still holds 100 companies. For an angel investor, these are really good stats, but nonetheless, it's still losing money in half of his deals.

The number of investments and amounts per investment

Many people ask what the magic number of companies that you should hold in your portfolio is. A number that will avoid being too concentrated, and a number that will avoid the troubles of dealing with an unmanageable portfolio, a portfolio where you can't add value. This will depend on your circumstances. On one level, on the amount of funds that you have ready to invest. Making investments of less than $25,000 if you have a view to add value to your companies, as the time you will be spending will not justify the skin you will have in the game.

Dan Martell tries to invest the same in each company and tries to assign to more than 12 companies at a time.

 Portfolio approach, meaning that if you only have half a million bucks, I think back when I started I had a couple million, so

whatever you want to allocate and deploy, try to do at least 12 investments. In my early days it was like 200,000 to my brother, hundred thousand to this other person, 25,000 to this person. It just makes no sense because essentially what you're doing with that capital allocation is you're trying to be predictors of success. And in tech and innovation where it's absolutely flip of the coin. You have to create a portfolio. It's like dollar cost averaging and buying into the market. So you want to do the same concept, so the same amount of capital, same timeline, whatever amount of dry powder you want to set aside to deploy. Make sure that you just write the same check size every time."

Coincidentally, Francisco Coronel, one of our distinguished angels, thinks similarly and supports it with some research done at HBS:

I think the minimum number of companies to invest in, in order to get a good diversification, is between 12 and 15 companies. In the angel investment approach, consider that 90% of the companies in that stage could fail, the failure rate is between 80 and 90%. So for 10 companies, if you put money in, you have a lot of chances to lose all the money. So I think in order to pick the winner, you have to create a 12 or 15 company portfolio.

According to research by Simonov from HBS, if you want to get a 50% chance to reach 2x return from your portfolio, you have to invest in at least 15 investments. He created some fundamentals of the investment thesis for angel investors and 500 Startups, the accelerator took these fundamentals in order to create his investment strategy. To invest a little money in 500 or 1000 startups. Then he created a follow on investment strategy, because of this correlation between as much as you diversify your portfolio, the probability to achieve a ROI between two and three x is higher."

To round up this topic, Jason Seats from Techstars is a great person to shed light, as his role allows him to see different people worldwide making decisions on investments each year. Techstar invests in 10 companies per location per year, and they have over 50 locations right now.

I get to observe 50 people making 10 startup portfolio investments every year for the last, you know, however long. What I can say with a pretty high level of confidence is that 10 companies is not sufficient diversification to bring down the variance of outcomes for a portfolio in an early stage venture. It's just because the volatility of the asset is so high. And so if your whole portfolio is 10 companies, more likely than not, you are going to either over perform, or underperform the typical expectation of venture capital. You need to be prepared for either end of that spectrum.

I think a more diversified sort of starting point would probably be closer to 30 companies, 25, 30 companies which is a lot. And so thinking about what's the size of a check that you would write if you want to invest in that many companies, or upfront acknowledge the fact that I am going to have a slightly more concentrated portfolio. I want to make 10 investments, but I am comfortable with the possible variants of that outcome and the fact that I may underperform or I may over perform. So, I'm reacting to the number 10. I think maybe 25, 30 is a better starting point. In terms of how you think about putting money into those companies. You can get different answers from every investor, I would say, especially if you're just starting out, resist that instinct to some extent and be a little bit more even with the way that you invest in these companies. Because you will likely be surprised by what works in that set and what doesn't work in that set. And also you'll be surprised at how they change over time. Six months in, three years in, five years in; the high flyers early sometimes don't go where you think they're going to go. The ones that are slow out of the gate sometimes end up being very dramatic successes. You don't have enough samples to see how to concentrate your investments.

So my recommendation would be 25 plus positions, roughly the same amount in each and observe. Then if you want to invest more into it than that amount of money, have some money set aside and have a plan for what percentage of these companies you would think you'd want to put more and maybe half of them, maybe a quarter of them. Just have a little bit of a formula about this that you want to do a second check that looks like twice the first check or something in that next round or whatever else. That's how I think about it, but I'm certain you'll get different answers from different people. So it's worth hearing all those answers before you come up with your plan"

Should your portfolio be invested across different sectors?

We recommend new angels to invest in a few sectors with a connection in order to create synergy value in the portfolio. Investing across different sectors is okay to create diversification and lower the impact of certain events happening in the economy. However, investing in a specific sector makes an angel more professional, more of an expert in that sector. And the potential to add value and create differentiation from other angel investors is much more important if you are more focused on one sector.

Francisco Coronel adds to this line of thought:

If your portfolio is over diversified, you could get only average asset returns. Moreover, portfolio management is difficult if you have too many investments. The risk is sometimes increased when a portfolio is widely diversified, because the investor invests in many companies that they know little or even nothing about. Another aspect is the transaction cost. If you invest funds in too many companies, the transaction costs could become a high percentage of your whole investment strategy."

Another of our ambassadors, Eneko Knörr, shows us that you can be successful by investing across different industries. In his case, his strongest point is being extremely well-connected in his geography, which makes him a constant target for talented Spanish entrepreneurs:

 There are investors that are very, very focused on a small niche or something they're basing in their expertise. I mean, it sounds like someone that comes from, you know, sports world so they invest only in sport or in sport tech. But in my case, my thesis is very broad, so I invest in anything related to technology, could be B2C, B2B. I invested in a lot of totally different things I'm thinking now. For instance, until now I never invested in health until two months ago that I invested in a company related to health. But my scope is very broad. I understand that it could be a good idea for an investor to be specialised in something. But on the other hand you may miss a lot of opportunities, because you're not investing in other areas. So this is something to take into account. I don't know, it depends on every investor and on every person."

Diversification

Diversification is the process of allocating capital in a way that reduces the exposure to any one particular asset or risk. Volatility is reduced by investing in a variety of assets.

Diversification is essential for investing in early-stage startups as an asset. And the reason why is because the outcomes are so incredibly volatile. More than half the time, investments are not going to work out. And so beyond just psychologically and emotionally preparing yourself for that, you have to mathematically prepare yourself. It means that a very small number of things you invest in will make up all of that difference. Now, when you add it all up, as a group, those investments, when you have enough of them, tend to do well.

Jason Seats, CIO from Techstars, contributes:

In order to do well, you have to do enough for your startups that you have a high enough likelihood of getting exposure to the ones that are massive outperformers. Diversification is essential to that. Because of diversification, I think it actually would be pretty hard to invest enough just in your area of domain expertise. So you will have to likely branch from that or understand how to expand on that in tangential ways. For me as an angel investor, I actually viewed my early investments as education. Education both in how this works and I don't know what mistakes I'm going to make. And so I just expected every investment I made was going to be a total loss and then I was paying for an expensive education. But I also learned about different industries. The areas that I feel comfortable evaluating companies now are much broader than what they were 10 years ago when I started because I've invested in lots of different companies. I've invested in ad tech companies or

healthcare companies or transportation, all things that I would not have known about before. But you learn about them via the investments. And so if you factor that in, you're getting an education at the same time."

Fabrice Grinda is a bit more extreme in his approach to diversification. He suggests:

 Invest in a lot of deals. If you invest in less than 10 deals, you're going to lose money. To make money you probably need to invest in more than 50 deals, there's a huge amount of luck in angel investing, which companies make or don't make it just because finding product market fit, defeating your competition. The diversification is absolutely key. So I would say at least 50 investments is what you need to actually have a proper portfolio."

Developing an investment thesis

Investment theses have been very common to see in venture capitalist firms, but we see more and more angels that create their own and publish it publicly. An investment thesis explains a particular investment strategy based on analysis, research, and logical ways of thinking.

In the venture capital world, a general partner, or what we call GP, prepares a formal document, which is an investment thesis, to show other potential investors how they are planning to deploy funds after a fundraising round. We believe that creating an investment thesis is a good exercise for angel investors. In order to create one, a vision into the future and interpreting the market dynamics is key.

An angel has to be clear about the main aspects of an investment thesis. For example, the stage of growth of the startup they are looking into, whether they are investing in the companies that are in a concept or in the market validation phase, or in the expansion of their business. There are different stages for different investment theses and different sectors or different regions in different countries. So, it is very important for an angel investor to consider different aspects of the potentiality of different investments according to the basics of an investment thesis.

Building a pipeline
When should you exit?
When should you top up your investment?

How to create an investment thesis

It can be quite easy to establish certain criteria for your investments, like the size of the company you want to see and the amount you spend on each deal. However, it is not easy to decide which will be the winning sectors of the future, and within those sectors, what will actually happen. A bit of futurology might be required. An expert in this field, Fabrice Grinda, gives his take on how he does it:

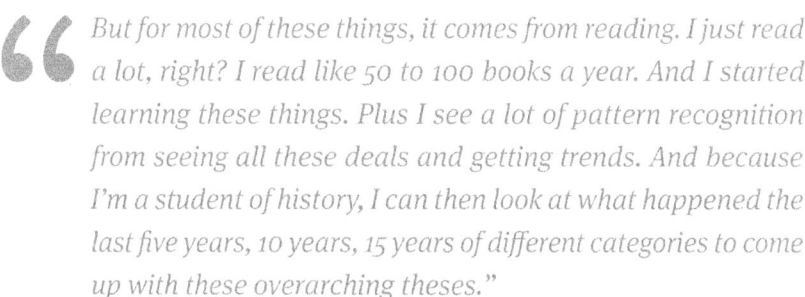

> *But for most of these things, it comes from reading. I just read a lot, right? I read like 50 to 100 books a year. And I started learning these things. Plus I see a lot of pattern recognition from seeing all these deals and getting trends. And because I'm a student of history, I can then look at what happened the last five years, 10 years, 15 years of different categories to come up with these overarching theses."*

So read a lot, see a lot of deals, and study history.

Still needing inspiration?

Our ambassador Alexander Jarvis has compiled a vault full of investment theses by different venture capitalist firms. We are displaying one from Adam Benayoun from 500 startups in Israel here, but there are many more online in Alexander's website.

> **Basics**
>
> ✓ **Location:** Israeli companies or companies founded by Israeli founders.
>
> ✓ **When:** As soon as you have a product and early market validation.
>
> ✓ **How much:** $50k-$100k initial check as part of a larger seed round.
>
> ✓ **What:** B2B, developer tools, SaaS, and marketplaces startups.
>
> ✓ **Who:** 2-3 founders with at least one technical founder.

Team

I believe the team is what leads a startup to succeed or fail. Here's what I'm looking for in a team:

> ✓ **Customer focused:** They care about their customers and are genuinely interested in making their life easier.
>
> ✓ **Cohesive:** A team that has worked long enough together to know how to handle differences and that are complementing each other. Preferably ego free.
>
> ✓ **Determined yet coachable:** Looking for the right blend of resiliency, persistency, determination, and the ability to listen to others.
>
> ✓ **Good people:** I want to back good and moral people.

Market

- ✓ **Large addressable market:** The addressable market (TAM) has to be at least a couple of hundred of millions of $ and grow reasonably fast every year.

- ✓ **Competition:** A market without competitors raises a flag, while a crowded market will be less than ideal since I'm always worried that it will end with a race to the bottom. However this can be countered by having a **unique** and a well **differentiated** product that drives substantial value to customers.

Other points

- ✓ I'll try to make a quick and informed decision but when I can't form an opinion in a timely manner, expect my decision not to invest.

- ✓ I'll be as candid as possible with my feedback – I don't like evasive answers or sugarcoating reality. If you won't take it well, then maybe we weren't a good fit to start with.

- ✓ Even if I say no, keep me posted about your progress. 99% of the time I'm wrong, and I like to be proven wrong. If you made significant progress that warrants taking a second look – please send me an email."

When to exit your investments

Different angels will recommend very different strategies when it comes to exit. Some like to capitalize on gains as soon as they can and move on to further investments. For example, Paloma Cabello likes to exit as soon as there is a good return in order to have cash for the next investment opportunity:

> *I exit startups when another investor comes in. To sell your investment, you do a hybrid deal where there is cash in and cash out. The new investor will buy the new shares, but also old shares. Sometimes the investors don't want you to leave, which is a tricky thing because they trust the fact that you are there and they want you there. Then you will need to make another different deal, maybe an anti-dilution or whatever. But typically they are happy to see you go. They want to be on their own."*

Others will look at holding for as long as possible, like Dan Scheinman.

This is a very illiquid type of investing. It takes a long time to build a meaningful outcome. And when you think about portfolio construction, an angel should be prepared for seven, eight years of money moving one direction before it starts to slow and potentially reverse. Venture funds, as an example, typically are 10 to 12-year structures.

As a very illiquid asset to invest in, investors have to be prepared for that. On any individual startup, you don't have that many opportunities to sell. It's not the same as buying a stock in the stock market or even owning commercial real estate where you would decide to put it on the market. It's not easy to just put your shares in these illiquid early-stage private companies on the market.

For any given company, there are typically 10 or less actual transaction opportunities over the lifetime of that business, times when you could either be a buyer or seller of shares. It's rare that there is a selling opportunity. So when you have a selling opportunity, how do you think about what your action should be? Should I sell? Should I hold? Should I maybe be a buyer at this moment? In general, selling or holding are the best opportunities.

Probably, it's been a long time since you made your investment, and the startup has matured. And so, how do you decide if you want to hold or sell? A simple hybrid approach might work well in this case, such as selling a portion of the shares, especially for companies worth 100 million dollars to a billion dollars in private value. For example, Techstars, when they have organic liquidity opportunities, will typically think about selling a quarter to half of their position, hedging their risk. If you sell half your position at that point, no one will think you are a total idiot; at most, everyone thinks you're half of an idiot. And if things have worked out really well, you're banking a win. You're getting liquidity, but you're still letting something ride, and you get a little bit of the best of both worlds. We believe this is a great approach, especially for you as a potential new angel investor.

This hedging approach is useful for training purposes too. It allows investors to still see what happens with the final outcome of that business; you're still part of that story and can watch the ultimate outcome. This means waiting until secondary and private liquidity opportunities arise or when a company goes public and the shares become tradable. At that point, I would say you're out of this sphere. You own a public asset, and you should think about that the same way you think about trading stocks. And so, if you're an angel investor, you're probably done at that point unless those shares sort of fit your public investing strategy.

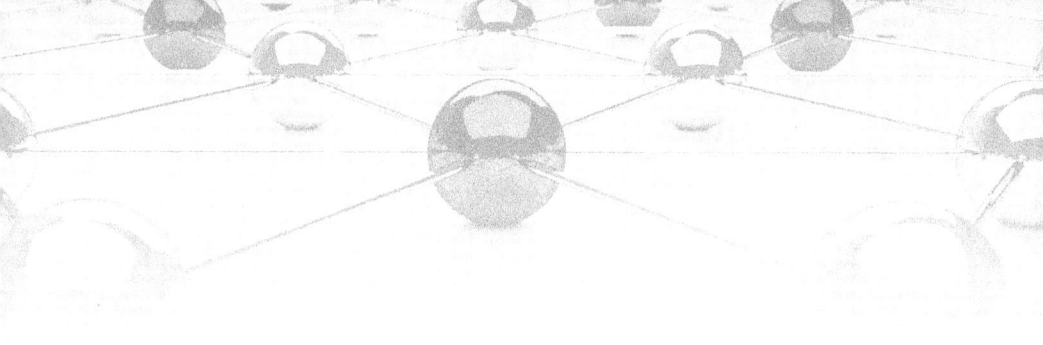

SECTION SEVEN

Investing as Team - Syndicate, and Others

A great way to start your angel adventure, especially when you are not sure how to source or analyze deals, is through one of the many ways available out there to co-invest and learn from others. To start building your reputation and your portfolio you do not necessarily have to come from single angel deals. It is becoming more and more common to co-invest, so researching the different options is a great first step.

The main options outside of individual deals are essentially:

1. Syndicates and angel associations
2. Crowdfunding
3. Angel Clubs
4. Funds, SPACs, and VCs

We will look in detail at each and discuss the pros and cons of each at any given stage of your investment journey.

Syndicates

One of the most common ways to invest when you are starting or further along the line is syndicates.

A syndicate is a union or association of individuals or businesses that collaborate to manage significant investments that may be too large for one individual. The purpose of syndicates is often to spread the risk.

Hence, an angel syndicate is a group of angel investors working together to provide financial backing for startups or entrepreneurs. Each angel would therefore contribute a smaller amount of money than if they were investing directly in the company. This allows angels to invest in more companies and achieve better diversification. Syndicates are especially valuable when angels are starting, when they don't have that much capital to deploy or not enough time to perform due diligence but want to start investing. This allows angels to avoid putting all their money in the same company or a few companies.

The primary difference between syndicates and other angel groups is that syndicates have what is known as a "lead investor." This person will lead the investment selection and provide the biggest check. Additionally, syndicates are usually formed by investors who have vast industry and business experience. They receive high-rate business deals and have better deal flow.

The lead investor or the person arranging the syndicate usually receives a fee, which can either be upfront and/or a percentage or "carry" on all successful investments (more about carry below). Syndicates usually attract more angel investors due to their track records and experience and manage to raise more funds for startups than individual investors.

Finding the winning startups is hard to come by as individuals, but syndicates usually have networks of VCs, investors, and entrepreneurs. This allows them to find the winning startups more often.

The better networks, combined with their experience and knowledge to carry out more comprehensive due diligence, will increase the odds of investing in a successful startup.

These syndicate groups are springing up all over the world, but as we have in every game, there are big players, and there are bigger players.

The biggest syndicate place online is AngelList, it is the most popular syndicate hub. Other syndicates that you might consider are Leva, FundersClub, SyndicateRoom, and The Syndicate.

To participate in some of these groups, you may need a personal connection because they are mainly by invitation only. In some cases, groups allow prospects to attend meetings to observe and contribute; this helps the members measure their commitment level and what they can add to the team.

Some groups might require annual subscriptions or membership fees. These groups also hold periodic events where they invite startups and entrepreneurs in need of finance to come and pitch their ideas and businesses. These may be great opportunities to meet people and network, regardless of the amount you end up investing through the syndicate.

Purpose of investing as team

Team investment gives the startups and entrepreneurs confidence in securing funding for their ideas or business. It also boosts the investor's position, knowing he is not alone in trusting his funds in a particular startup or business. Angel investors form teams for various reasons, some of which are:

- √ To lower the risk level when investing in startups
- √ Being a member of a group helps to conduct better due diligence

✓ The team have access to control deal flow

✓ Teams have the resources to increase portfolio diversification as the combined networks will be larger than each individual's network on their own

✓ To have more control to manage the success of the startups they have invested in

Where and how to find angel investor syndicates

You can find investor syndicates almost everywhere these days, depending on your industry and your location (although many syndicates operate online too). Some are more open and general, while others focus on specific industries. Syndicate investors have provided financing backing for more than 60,000 U.S startups and entrepreneurs.

Depending on your research, connections, or network, there are different ways to find angel investor groups:

Internet

The internet is loaded with information on how to find angel investor groups. You can search geographically, and according to the industry you play in or search for general investor groups. AngelList is one such online platform that allows you to create your syndicate groups or join an existing one. Tools such as Crunchbase, PitchBook, LinkedIn, and others will undoubtedly help you find the right groups to invest in.

Angel investor associations

The US Angel Capital Association has a comprehensive online directory of angel investor groups. The same applies to other countries; you only need to know how to find what you are looking for in terms of your investment thesis, your interests, or your passion.

Networking

As mentioned in Section Two, networking is the best way to find startups and other investors, as well as finding angel investor syndicates. Being a member of an industry association can be greatly beneficial when checking out syndicate angel investors.

Introduction by other members

Some syndicates have stringent requirements for adding new members, and one such requirement is "membership by invitation only."

In this case, a new member can only join the group by an existing member's invitation.

Pitching events

Pitching events where entrepreneurs and startups meet with investor groups to discuss their ideas and businesses is another great avenue to find and introduce yourself to the managers of angel syndicates.

Suppose you are an investor interested in joining such a syndicate. In that case, the pitching event is a great avenue to make your interest known to other investors present.

Some pitching events are nowadays held online. This is also a great way to spend less time (since there is no travel time) but still get a chance to meet the founders and other interested investors. It will be slightly harder at the beginning, but keeping in touch and talking regularly with the people you meet will make it much easier.

Benefits of syndicates to startups

Sometimes you will find that many founders and startups approach syndicates first and later try to fill funding rounds with individual angels directly. So how do startups and entrepreneurs benefit from syndicates, or why would startups choose syndicates instead of individual angel investors or groups?

Below are some of the advantages startups stand to gain from working with syndicates compared to individual angel investors.

Larger and more efficient funding

Startups get to enjoy a more streamlined process of funding for their businesses or ideas. Hence, they can provide more considerable funding for startups at the early stages than individual investors. The benefit to startups is massive because they will have access to funding without fear or limitation.

Syndicates will also have a more efficient process of allocating funds and closing the round. For example, the syndicate will set deadlines for investors and take care of the due diligence for the individual investors, as only the syndicate will technically be facing the startup. This means that the startup will not have to chase individual investors to wire the funds or check references, a process that usually takes a long time to complete.

Capitalization table

As we have seen, the cap-table is the document that shows who the shareholders of a company are. So unless you are a known angel, there is little interest in the startup to have many names in their cap table for small amounts. That means they need to send reports, deal with many names in succeeding funding rounds, and there is potential of risks involved in future rounds as many shareholders mean potential voting issues. Syndicates solve this issue by grouping all shareholders under one name, and therefore all admin and voting issues have a single point of contact.

Wider resources

In addition to more significant funding from syndicates, startups benefit from the massive resources available in a syndicate. These resources come in the form of industry experience, skills, contacts, expertise, among others. Startups who work with individual investors are likely to experience some limitations in these resources.

With syndicates, a startup gets a bigger pool of resources. It is more than just mentorship from the lead investor and the backers from different backgrounds and expertise that startups can tap from. Although there is usually one point of contact, nothing keeps other angels from getting involved with the startup and offering their help, even if they have invested as part of a syndicate.

Startups can stay focused.

Dealing with syndicates makes the fundraising process easy for business owners and startups. The lead syndicate is primarily responsible for all the paperwork and fundraising exercises. Business owners will not have to manage numerous investors.

Dealing with only the lead investor almost helps move the process faster than if you have to deal with individuals or members in other angel groups.

How the syndicate process works

Investments come in different sizes, so do the syndicates. The rules of engagement are also not the same, which could be due to the size of the startup's funding or its complexity.

No rules or conditions are binding the angels in a syndicate. In general terms, though, investors are bound by a gentleman's agreement that has been put in place to guide how the group will function. Moreover, payments will likely be made through funds or investment vehicles arranged at low costs in order to formalize the agreements.

Here's how it works on paper:

Opening phase

The lead syndicate selects a startup they believe has fantastic upside potential. These selections would naturally happen after a series of pitches and, in some cases, after being approached by startups or founders.

After their due diligence, the lead then extends the opportunity to the group, offering pertinent data linked to the transaction. The lead investor is likely to have made up their mind and committed a certain amount. Information including the amount involved, valuation, company structure, timing of the operation and deadlines, general terms of the offer, fees involved, etc., are some of the common details that the lead investor will communicate in order to get the deal done.

Investment deal

Members interested in the startup or operating in the same industry know how to find more details about the startup and the founders.

As an interested investor, you could ask for more information about the offer. The lead investors will offer all pertinent details to assess the investment opportunity correctly and will liaise with the founders. Some of this information about the business includes business design, milestones reached, industry size, staff, financial information, and term sheet.

Interested investors will then specify the amount they are willing to invest. In some instances, the lead investor suggests the amount the syndicate should invest.

Next is the commitment to invest by signing some documents like an investment agreement, duration, and terms and conditions where the risk and returns are spelled out. The lead syndicate will handle all these on behalf of the group. The documents that are typically reviewed are a Limited Partnership Agreement, which explains the company that has been setup to invest in the startup, the Subscription Agreement, which explains the terms at which you are buying shares, and a Private Placement Memorandum or

PPM, in short, a legal document that explains the summary of the offering, risks, description of securities, use of proceeds and other important details.

Closing the deal

To make the deal process smoother, an investment vehicle is created. It will be responsible for taking care of all the bottlenecks involved in the process.

Depending on the terms, the investment vehicle's expenses will either be shared or paid by the agreed party irrespective of the financial backing the syndicate is providing.

Finally, once the investment vehicle has completed its task of ensuring all angles are covered, the lead investors ensure the funds are transferred to the startup. In some instances, the fund is assigned to an escrow where the investment vehicle monitors the fund's management.

Tracking

At this next phase, the lead syndicate will be responsible for tracking the investment, meeting with the startups, and updating the group with information about the startup's progress and performance.

Termination of investment

No investor likes to see this, but sometimes it can happen. If the investment is not going well, the lead syndicate and the startup can agree to terminate the deal. This could be a result of a total or partial acquisition of the startup.

If this happens, the syndicate will get back its investment, dividends, and capital gains, if any. The lead syndicate will also be paid a certain percentage or carry, if there are any gains above the initial investments and any other specified hurdles. Carry can vary, but it is usually around 20%, and hurdle rates are roughly at 6% per annum.

As a practical example, let's assume an investor has invested $10,000 into the syndicate of Startup X with a carry rate of 20% and a hurdle rate of 6% per annum. If Startup X is liquidated after two years and the valuation is now 2x what it was when they invested, an investor will receive their initial capital of $10,000 plus $1200 in interest (hurdle rate). The remaining $8800 from the liquidation of the shares will be shared with the lead investor in the syndicate at a rate of 80% and 20% meaning individual investors will receive $7040 and the lead investor $1740 (assuming no other fees).

Syndicate structure and cost

Syndicates are nowadays more accessible to startups, founders, and investors. Suppose you are an investor interested in investing alongside other angels on different deals. In that case, you can set up a syndicate and define the structure by which the group operates.

Platforms like AngelList have simplified the formation and participation in a syndicate. You can either join an existing group or start something of your own. There are other platforms where you can only be a backer if you are an accredited investor.

It's free to gain access to investing on AngelList. However, some portion is retained to cover setup, management, or administrative fees when investors invest. These fees are specific to each Fund or Syndicate and are explained during the closing process. Additionally, suppose the investment returns a profit. In that case, a portion of that profit or carry is retained by the fund lead or the investment advisor, as mentioned before.

While it is mainly free to join a syndicate (bar some exceptions), fees are associated with the setup, management, and administration of deals when members invest.

Special Purpose Vehicle (SPV)

The Special Purpose Vehicle is created for every deal. SPVs allow early-stage investors to raise funds for late-stage pro-rata and unique opportunities.

The example below is a standard syndicate structure.

A syndicate is investing $184,000 in a startup called Zeba Inc.

The setup fee is $16,000, while Carry is 20% with no hurdle rate.

Hence the syndicate will be raising $200,000 to achieve a $184,000 investment in Panther Inc. (subtracting the setup fee).

The group gets $20,000 investment each from 10 members, with each member covering 10% of the setup fee. That means from the $20,000 invested by each member, $1,600 is set aside for setup fees while $18,400 goes to Panther Inc.

A few years down the line, Panther Inc. attracts a buyer who buys over the company, and the syndicates get a $1,000,000 payout.

At this point, each investor will get back their investment of $20,000 each (10% of the $200,000). From what is left, which is $800,000, 20% ($160,000) will be set aside as carry, and the balance of $640,000 will be distributed to the ten investors.

The final position for each of the ten investors will look as follows:

- ✓ Initial investment $20,000

- ✓ Add 10% of $640,000, which is the share of the amount left after deducting carry ($800,000 - $160,000). $64,000

- ✓ Total Payout to each investor on this deal is $84,000 ($20,000 + $64,000).

Note how carry was not mentioned or treated until after the deal turned profitable.

Traditional fund

Naturally, investors pay a management fee and carry to the fund lead. Carry is usually around 20%, while management is around 2%.

For instance:

Say $2,000,000 with 10 investors and each contributing $200,000.

The lead will receive $40,000 as a 2% management fee. The investor pays $4,000 (10% of $40,000) with $196,000 left for the investible fund.

If the fund generates and reports positive returns, and $2,000,000 is due to be distributed. The investors will get back their initial investment of $200,000 and 80% of what is left after deducting carry (80% of $1,800,000).

The amount to be distributed is:
   Amount declared for distribution $2,000,000
   Deduct initial investment $200,000 = $1,800,000
   Less Carry 20% ($360,000) of $1,800,000 = $1,440,000
   The amount each member gets $144,000
   Final take home for each member (Invested Amount + Return on Investment)
   $200,000 + $144,000 = $344,000

Lead investing in syndicates

Lead syndicates are angels with experience and deep knowledge in choosing investment opportunities and investing in various businesses and deal flows that many investors do not have access to. Their networks are usually strong and the main source of deals. They are inclined to be angels or productive startup founders who've been a part of various industries for a long time and understand the intricacies.

Functions of a syndicate lead

A syndicate lead is an essential part of any angel syndicate and helps the group to speak and act as one unit. Their function could include:

- ✓ Organizing the activities of the syndicate. This includes carrying out due diligence and also leading negotiations and agreements.
- ✓ They are responsible for finding additional angels if necessary.
- ✓ The lead is responsible for monitoring the group's investment. This consists of acting as the link between the syndicate, the investors, and the startup.
- ✓ The lead syndicate would typically function as the investor best positioned to operate with the investee, considering the time and experience he has to offer. He will probably have built a fantastic working relationship with all the startups or founders while acting as a direct investor before the deal is completed.
- ✓ Having a lead investor working with the startups gives the backers the confidence to do more. The lead usually has the skills and experience to carry out thorough due diligence on intending business deals.

Startups will naturally do better working with a lead syndicate than working with single investors. This is so because groups come with more experience and the willingness to centralize an efficient communication channel.

Qualities of a lead syndicate

There are some core qualities that every syndicate leader needs to possess; the top among these qualities are:

Good track record: This involves angels with a good track record investing in startups, as well as following on and exiting. Or founders with access to the financing required to invest in startups.

Access to funding: Lead investors will be required to invest in the companies they choose for the group. Put your money where your mouth is.

Good deal flow: A lead must know how to find exclusive deals regularly for the group to invest in.

Good startup sense: A good lead syndicate must possess good judgment, and it comes from a vast knowledge of the market and the experience necessary to make the right call on deals.

A lead investor may readily satisfy all of those qualities and might still not lock down a successful deal. Investing in startups of any sort always brings with it its fair share of risk. However, syndicate investing can help reduce this risk as your individual amounts will be lower, diversification higher, and you will invest following a trusted and experienced investor.

Crowdfunding

As the name implies, crowdfunding is when a crowd funds a project or business instead of venture capital or a few individuals. This can be relevant to people that are interested in learning about early-stage investments.

Our ambassador Bill Morrow explains:

> *Crowdfunding is normally for companies that can attract angel funding. And the distinction between those two is that the principle of crowdfunding is based on the wisdom of the crowd. Over the years, I genuinely haven't seen much wisdom. Crowdfunding platforms are an excellent mechanism to give founders who either don't have the self-awareness to understand that they need something more than money or who just want money for a short-term gain, an excellent mechanism to do that. But I think if you look at the longevity, the sustainability of companies that have founded or raised money on crowdfunding platforms, it's really low."*

Crowdfunding is another form of alternative finance and crowdsourcing. It's the practice of raising small amounts of money from many interested investors to finance a project. Crowdfunding is primarily done via the internet, where there's easy accessibility to a vast network of investors.

Crowdfunding sites bring entrepreneurs and investors together, with the capability to raise entrepreneurship by enlarging the pool of investors beyond the conventional group of relatives, owners, and venture capitalists.

To conduct a successful crowdfunding campaign, you have to catch the interest of a high number of both backers and convince them that your business is worthy of the investment.

Types of crowdfunding

Crowdfunding is divided into four types, but the typical quality in all four is they all receive money from members of the public and mainly through the internet and specified platforms such as Kickstarter, Indiegogo, Seedrs, and Crowdcube.

Crowdfunding can be done for raising equity, debt, donations as well as rewards.

Let's look at each one and examples.

Donations

The donation type of crowdfunding occurs when people contribute to a campaign, a business, a movement, or an individual expecting nothing in return. This type of crowdfunding can be likened to contributing toward a charitable cause.

Assuming you create a crowdfunding campaign for the public to help your company purchase a particular machine type to speed up manufacturing. The people who provided you with cash to buy this machine offer their support for your company's expansion and nothing else. They would neither get their money back nor get any form of interest.

GoFundMe

GoFundMe.com is an example of a donation-based crowdfunding firm. Though it's mainly employed for charitable initiatives, companies have benefited from the platform. This is a superb alternative for nonprofit organizations like NGOs and companies that have service-based industries.

Other donation crowdfunding platforms are Fundly, DonorsChoose, and Causes.

Debt

Debt-based crowdfunding is also called peer-to-peer (P2P) financing, which is a kind of crowdfunding. In debt-based crowdfunding, the money pledged by backers is a loan that must be repaid with interest on a particular deadline. Businesses use this type of campaign to raise funds from the public for a specific time. The percentage interest on the invested amount is specified, so is the date of paying back the principal and interest.

Other debt-based crowdfunding platforms are Prosper, LendingClub, FundingCircle, and P2BInvestor.

LendingClub

LendingClub is a debt-based crowdfunding website since it's a P2P lending platform. It provides around $40,000 in private loans as well as $500,000 in small business funding. Each loan duration is three or five years.

To be eligible, your organization must have already been in operation for at least a calendar year. The applicant should own at least 20% of the firm. It needs to have a yearly sales revenue of $50,000.

Reward

A reward-based crowdfunding campaign offers the backers something in return for their investment. These rewards may be based on each contribution's size or may come in services, products, discounts, branded products, and others.

Kickstarter

Kickstarter is the most popular rewards-based crowdfunding platform that has been helping companies since 2009. It has been used to raise over $5 billion for over 182,000 projects. Kickstarter is generally successful because it has a simple platform. All you need to do is specify your financial need and the time you have to reach it in your campaign. Then share your project with the community in hopes of finding a backer.

Other reward-based crowdfunding platforms are Indiegogo and RocketHub.

Equity

Equity-based crowdfunding enables small companies and startups to give away a part of their company in exchange for financing. These contributions are an investment in which participants get shares in the company based on their investment size. The investor receives ownership in the company in return for their investment.

Equity Crowdfunding Platforms - CircleUp, Fundable, Crowdcube, and MicroVentures.

Currently, in the United States, equity crowdfunding isn't merely readily available for accredited but also for non-accredited Investors.

Previously non-accredited investors were not legally able to invest in equity crowdfunding, but following President Obama's signing of the JOBS Act in April of 2012, non-accredited investors can now legally participate in equity crowdfunding.

The challenges of crowdfunding

Many people assume crowdfunding is a simple or completely free means of raising money, but it demands a great deal of effort to set a project that backers will perceive as "worth the support." Success is not guaranteed, and since crowdfunding continues to gain recognition, backers are wiser in the projects they support.

Crowdfunding functions for many organizations in many different phases, but the businesses with the most prosperous campaigns tend to possess the greatest and most participated communities supporting them, usually clients or customers or other fans of the goal.

Creating a campaign that would generate this kind of widespread support could be challenging. It requires a solid marketing campaign, reliable founders, and also a top-quality product. The challenges of crowdfunding are extensive.

Here are the significant challenges of crowdfunding:

- ✓ Getting and implementing a low-cost advertising plan before, during, and following crowdfunding effort
- ✓ Creating a message with the right tone in the description that will generate interest in the merchandise or service
- ✓ Producing an educational and exciting campaign video that explains the solution and its advantages. The most critical challenge is, it is expensive to create an ideal high-impact video
- ✓ Making and planning the rewards program to maximize the ROI strategically
- ✓ Deciding the effective and cost-efficient fulfillment strategy for the rewards
- ✓ When thinking of a crowdfunding campaign, these are just the basic challenges to worry about. There may be other challenges that are unique to your particular type of product or service.

For equity-based crowdfunding, there is the need to educate new people that many times have no background in investment, and at the same time, try not to bore the experienced investors.

Crowdfunding is like buying and selling online, which many people are already familiar with, especially if they have to pre-order and wait some months before the product is ready. However, people who are not conversant with angel investing and crowdfunding will need more convincing before they part with their funds.

Potential benefits of crowdfunding for new angel investors

Crowdfunding is usually not a profitable means of investing in startups. Plenty of crowdfunded projects tend to go to the crowds when they have no other means of fundraising. However, there have been some successful companies that recurred to crowdfunding as a way to market their company and get as many people involved with the company. For example, UK challenger bank Monzo has performed quite well in their crowdfunding campaign, raising over £20 million.

Like our ambassador Tom Britton points out:

 People talk about the Monzo raise and the Revolut raise, those are great examples of the companies that should use crowdfunding. You've got a brand, you kind of invigorate your existing audience a little bit by giving them a share in the business or allowing them to buy a share in the business, word spreads.

Everybody finds out about it and Monzo got 10s of thousands and Revolut got 10s of thousands of signups from their crowdfunding campaigns. I think that's a great example of when it works really well. But people don't talk about all the other times where it doesn't work well, where someone doesn't know what they're doing, they see something that looks kind of flashy. They believe all the hype that the founder is saying, they put money in and six months later, the company's out of money already, you're like, Oh, great. I think that is angel investing."

In any case, angel investors can benefit from startups looking for crowdfunding as it is a very inexpensive way to get access to plenty of deals for a very small amount of investment. You can read pitches, financial models, test products, and MVPs and get involved with companies that you would not normally have access to. The range of documentation and resources available is vast, and they are a fantastic way of gaining some experience in the startup world.

Investing in startups via crowdfunding is not necessary as you can have access to most documents without investing, but even investing tiny amounts of money would get you more interested and allow you to receive reports and news from the company. This will certainly engage you personally, so we would recommend having a go at a couple of companies, even if the amounts will sound too small.

Our ambassador Eneko Knörr likes this approach:

 For new Angels this is all about learning, reading, and learning by doing which you really have to start investing. So, one good way to start investing is to go to these crowdfunding platforms to invest like 100 euros on a company, 100 euros in another. Just to learn, is the best way to learn. And then when you get confident and you know more and you'll know more people and you'll get a better deals, so maybe you can start investing more money."

AngelList syndicate system

Angellist is a U.S. online platform for angel investors, startups, and job seekers willing to work with startups. Founded in 2010 by Naval Ravikant and Babak Nivi, the platform's mission is to help startups with talent and fundraising challenges. Initially, the website focused on tech startups in need of funding. However, in 2015, it started allowing other startups to raise funds from angel investors for free.

With billions in assets under management, 47 Unicorns, and more than 3,500 managed funds, Angels, V.C.s, and startups rely on AngelList for capital and funds management.

AngelList SPVs

AngelList syndicates are Special Purpose Vehicles (SPV) to make single investments. They provide a cloud-based service to manage SPVs for venture capital funds, family offices, angel groups, and individuals. Additionally, AngelList ensures that SPVs and the participating investors remain private and confidential in all circumstances.

It allows investors to create their own syndicate using their technology and access the audience of Angel.co. Yearly, there are more than 1500 deals done through more than one hundred syndicates.

You can find syndicates that specialize in special stages of investment, such as early, seed, and growth, as well as stage in terms of revenue generation (prelaunch, pre-revenue, post-revenue, profitability). You can also specify an industry and even special interests such as Blockchain or Female founders. You can evaluate the syndicates based on the number of deals they have done, follow-on rate, and investments by stage.

When looking at deals, you can analyze their pitch deck, review the minimum amount that you can invest, the type of round that is being raised, the amount that his being raised as SAFE, the pre-money capitalization, the allocation of the syndicate, the setup costs of the syndicate, and the carry.

How to invest in early-stage funds

One of the many ways to get access to multiple startups is to invest via funds. A fund or investment vehicle is a type of investment product where the money of several investors is pooled into an investment product and used to purchase specific assets that correspond to the fund's investment goals.

Many venture capital firms issue funds, and many other investment companies may provide diversified exposure to startups. These vehicles and funds may be a great opportunity if you are starting as an angel and want to see the investment decisions of "the big guys," for example. Or, even if you are an experienced angel, funds can be a great way to get exposure to a different industry, area, geography, or investment thesis that you don't master but would like to dip your toes in.

So once you have decided to invest in a particular area through a fund (or similar investment vehicle), the options may be overwhelming as there are plenty of venture capital firms issuing funds for various different purposes. There are two key participants within a VC fund: general partners (GP) and limited partners (LP). The GPs are the people in charge of managing the fund and making the investment decisions – selecting the startups, funding them, and working with them to help them grow. LPs are the external investors, the people, institutions, and organizations who provide the capital needed for those investments. Becoming a limited partner or LP is an important decision, so there are several things to consider.

There are many funds, but not all of them are accessible for all investors. Funds are usually open for a limited time and/or until the target funding is reached. Many funds are also for selected clients only, such as Family Offices or large institutions. For that reason, if you see and have access to a fund you like, you should act quickly.

We will now focus on the general principles you should follow when selecting a fund to invest in. We have broken it down into a general due diligence checklist, which could serve as a quick reference guide.

What is your strategy?

A good start is to think about what you want to get out of the fund. Which market, industry, geography, investment stage do you want to get access or exposure to? What is your investment timeline, how much money will you allocate to this specific market, what do you expect as a return?

These are all good questions to start off, and their answers will limit the availability of existing funds to invest. Once you select your strategy and narrow down the number of funds or fund managers, you can use the quick due diligence guide below to select the appropriate fund for you. This can or not fit within your investment thesis. If you invest in a fund, you will be leaving due diligence and the startup selection to a professional crew, so funds give you the option to step outside of your comfort zone and diversify into the unknown yet potentially rewarding realm.

General due diligence criteria for fund selection

Fund managers or general partners

Perhaps the most important thing to look at when selecting a fund or a VC are the General Partners (GPs). These are the people you are relying upon to make the investments and choose which will be the next unicorn you are invested in. There are many things that you can search for in a GPs, including investment track record, previous funds, successful exits, failed investments, location, and board of directors and advisors.

Most of these are self-explanatory, but we would like to highlight that, in our view, the past investments from the GPs can come from either past funds or private investments. It is not always easy to find accurate information about past investments, but you will always see how the GPs advertise the good (and sometimes the bad) investments. Tools such as Crunchbase or PitchBook may help verify some of the information, although the information is limited. In any case, references will always help when studying GPs.

Another area we would like to focus on is "location". Nowadays, and with COVID-19 in the midst of disrupting our lives, we still believe that location is important. This becomes a key component when the geography in the investment thesis (as mentioned below) is in areas where you need local expertise (mainly emerging markets). In these cases, we would insist that the GPs have boots on the ground wherever their thesis leads them.

Do have a look at Angel Investor School, where we have discussed plenty of incredibly interesting regions such as the Middle East, Africa, Israel, and Latin America, all of which have their particularities.

Investment thesis

When analyzing an investment thesis, you need to look into the geography, the industry, market and sector, the investment stage, the "Secret sauce" offered, the number of investments and diversification, and the exit strategy per investment.

As discussed in detail with Francisco Coronel, the investment thesis of a fund is of vital importance. As an angel investor, you too should have an investment thesis, but whenever you want to step out of your comfort zone, looking for the right fund that fits whatever you want exposure to starts with reviewing their investment thesis. This will be the one place where you can tell if this is the market, sector, geography, and investment stage you want to have exposure to.

Regarding the investment stage, as an angel investor, you will usually be drawn to deploy your angel capital in the first investment stages (pre-seed and seed). However, there is no reason why you shouldn't aim for better-established companies through a fund or vehicle.

Factors such as the "secret sauce" also become very relevant for certain investors and GPs. For example, there is no better angel or investor in marketplaces than Fabrice Grinda. His expertise and knowledge of this sector make him the go-to person when looking at marketplaces.

Regarding diversification, we have addressed this in our portfolio management section. However, we would stress again that diversification plays a truly important role in startup investing. This will also be important at a fund level, as you want to see that they are deploying the funds in a diversified way. You can also diversify in the number of funds, but that will depend on your investment strategy and the reason behind choosing a fund over the other potential vehicles.

Finally, it is important to look at the exit strategy of the fund. An exit strategy is a plan executed by a fund or an investor to terminate or liquidate their investment after meeting certain conditions. It is simply the plan an investor has put in place to get out of a fund.

It's imperative to check out the exit plan of a fund. Not all would be the same, as several will seem to exit their investments at a specific round to present a predetermined exposure.

Not all are the same, as many will look to exit their investments at a certain round in order to provide a specified exposure. For example, a fund may focus on early-stage or pre-seed investments and have a policy of exiting whenever the startups fundraise at Series A or B. This may be a good strategy as it limits risks and allows for re-investments into other companies. Other funds may have discretion over the exit or hold until IPOs or liquidity events.

Other considerations

We have listed the main things that you need to consider. However, you should also consider other things such as the potential to co-invest in the companies in the fund, potential to participate or add value in the target companies, size of the fund, term, fund's jurisdiction, company reports, and media attention, whether there is a responsive and flexible administrator, how the fund's governance works, and who are the other LPs

There are several other considerations to take into account, especially as an angel investor. We particularly like those funds where the GPs welcome and encourage the LPs to invest alongside them, should they wish to. The companies where the fund has invested will carry a high degree of due diligence and, if they happen to be interesting to yourself or you know the market/sector/geography, it may be an interesting idea to invest alongside the fund and/or engage the with the company to provide advice and become an integral part of them. Many funds will allow for co-investments without any upfront or carry fees (see below), so this is an added value.

You need to factor in how long it would take to get your money and the return on investment back. There are different time frames for investment objectives. You also need to know the choices you have, if any. Angel investments, as well as funds that invest in startups may be illiquid for many years, so bear this in mind.

The fund's jurisdiction also plays an important role, as you should research the tax and legal implications of investing in a certain location. Nowadays, most funds are established in "friendly" locations, but it's always a good idea to choose.

Furthermore, you want a responsible fund administrator who will provide timely answers to your questions and periodic updates to review the development of the startups and investments.

Costs

Funds costs come in three flavors: upfront costs, running costs, and carry. Although costs are usually standard, there may be cases where there are significant deviations you should be careful with. A standard fund will have between 1.5% and 2.5% running per annum management fees, and there may or may not be placement fees.

Moreover, funds usually have a "carry" percentage. Carried interest, or carry, in finance, is a share of the profits of an investment paid to the GP in excess of the amount that the manager contributes to the partnership. So, for example, if the carry is 25% and the fund returns 100% excess, the GPs will retain 25% of the profits over and above a hurdle rate, the minimum expected rate of return of an investment, and the LPs will receive 75% of the profits. This, although it may sound high, is the main incentive for GPs. Wherever you participate and decide to co-invest alongside the GPs (for the funds that allow this), there is usually no running fees nor carry interest.

Liquidity

Unlike ETFs or Mutual Funds, VC or startup funds do not have much liquidity. You may be able to sell your portion privately (provided the GPs and administrators allow it), but bear in mind that liquidity will usually come from sales or exits that the fund has. Therefore, it is important to note that: (i) your money will likely be locked for several years, and (ii) the fund's strategy in terms of exits is important and relevant.

Taxes

As with any investment, your capital gains will be subject to tax. It is important to consider tax relief that might be provided by certain funds, such as SEIS and EIS in the United Kingdom. You might also want to consider whether you are investing as an individual or as part of a business organization.

Always dig deep

These high-level and general criteria should help you narrow down your options and make a reasonable choice. However, it is always good to probe and research the particular funds individually, ask for references, and check as much as you can.

But remember, among the most important factors to consider is how your investment fits into your overall strategy. Bear in mind that the risks are extremely high within the startup world, so diversification should always be within your strategy as one good investment may compensate for all other losses. This is what most funds focus on, rather than selecting a handful of startups to invest in.

Angel groups or clubs

Angel clubs or groups are groups of angel investors who share common interests and meet regularly to discuss potential opportunities in the startup world and often invest as a group. They share the deals that each receives through their network and agree to invest or not invest. Angels within the groups will discuss their own due diligence, and their experience in a specific industry or market will serve to test the different problems and solutions they come across presented by startups seeking funding.

Every group will have their own practices, rules, and ways of gathering, but the idea is simple: bring deals to the table to discuss their potential and invest (or refrain from investing) in startups. This should be an environment in which collaboration and freedom of speech should be cherished and where every member should feel free to express their opinion and bring in deals, whether they are bad or good in principle and whether or not they seem to have potential.

The groups usually focus on a geography or region, and in some cases, cities. However, with the development of online meeting tools, nowadays, clubs or groups span worldwide, and geography is no longer a boundary.

Groups may also form with a specific industry or market in mind or a target market where the members have expertise and connections.

The objective of groups and clubs is to leverage the individual members' expertise, access, networks, and funds to find and fund good startups.

They will usually invest at the pre-seed and seed stages, but that doesn't mean that either the club or group or the individual angels may not follow on with investments into Series A and beyond.

In terms of numbers, there are angel groups worldwide, with over 200 in the United States of America alone.

But not all is perfect around groups or clubs, as there have been some issues with them and therefore you should take note of these before you join them. For example, groups can lead to very long discussion and evaluation periods, long due diligence, plenty of repeated questions to the founders, discussion over investment terms, small check sizes, etc. So some startups are reluctant to accept or raise through angel groups. This is somewhat different from syndicates as syndicates will have a lead, and there is not much discussion; either angels like the deal and invest in the agreed terms or don't and walk away. Groups may delay the decision as the money is usually shared, and there is no lead figure. Also, a group environment may mean that some angels are not learning or gaining sufficient exposure to the startups, and many may feel shy to speak up or use their networks to find startups or help them out when invested.

In any case, we do recommend that you look into the groups of angels you may have around you and try to contribute and test whether this is something you enjoy or if you prefer to invest by yourself.

Active angel investment groups

There are hundreds of Angel groups available globally and plenty in your city. We highly encourage that you seek and join them, as we have discussed as part of the networking section. Angel Capital Association has a detailed directory of accredited and affiliate angel groups and platforms in the U.S. and Canada.

Beauhurst used the table below to rank 23 active angel groups in the U.K. This ranking is primarily based on equity deals completed between 1st quarter 2011 and 3rd quarter 2020. These deals were officially announced, while others were made known to the author.

This ranking should be taken as indicators only because many investors do not announce their deals to the public.

Ranking	Angel Network	No. of Deals Completed
1	Envestors	169
2	24Haymarket	123
3	Equity Gap	106
4	Archangels	103
5	Cambridge Angels	91
6	London Business Angels (managed by Newable)	89
7	TRICAPITAL	72
8	Kelvin Capital	56
9	QVentures	49
10	Dragons' Den (managed by the BBC)	48
11	Oxfordshire Investment Opportunity Network (managed by Oxford Innovation)	45
12	Angels Den	40
13	Cambridge Capital Group	34
14	Ascension Ventures Syndicate Club	31
15	Clearly Social Angels (managed by ClearlySo)	29
16	Highland Venture Capital	28
17	Bristol Private Equity Club	25
18	GC Angels	25
19	Green Angel Syndicate	25
20	London & Scottish Investment Partners	25
21	Minerva Business Angel Network (managed by University of Warwick Science Park)	23
22	Newable Ventures	22
23	Gabriel Investment Syndicate	22

SECTION EIGHT

Life as an Angel Investor

So you have already signed your first check, and now you are asking yourself what comes next. In this chapter, we look at your life as an angel investor. We also look at those heroes that have taken a long-term commitment to "angeling", breathing startup ideas, and investing in the future. Some may have already retired from day-to-day managerial roles, and others decide to invest themselves fully into angel investing or even grow into or join a venture capital firm as general partners.

Let's start by looking at the idea of being a full-time angel.

Can you be a full-time angel investor?

People that dive straight into investing and create their own seed fund may be perceived as venture capitalists rather than angel investors. They spend their time in meetings with prospective investments, mentoring founders from the companies that they partly own, raising money from LPs, getting involved in due diligence, negotiating deals, and so forth.

As an individual angel, you will be limited by the amount of time that you have. Even if you are relatively fast at doing your due diligence, the process of screening startups, meeting founders, and performing due diligence will take a toll on your energy and the number of companies that you can invest in and later add value to.

Individual angels that are fully committed can take between 10 to 20 companies on board a year. If on average they are deploying $25,000 per deal, this would mean they would be investing between $250,000 and $500,000 per year on a yearly basis. If they were doing this as a VC and took a management fee of 4%, this would mean that the fee they are charging for their work is $10,000 to $20,000, certainly not a lot for a person that can invest those amounts. Their opportunity cost is huge, and having a paid salary could bring in 10x-20x more, to say the least.

According to Bill Morrow, one of our ambassadors:

> *Economically, you can only give wisdom to six companies, 12 companies at an absolute maximum a year as an individual, whilst being a successful businessman and running a portfolio of your real business, which is actually where you've got the money there in the first place."*

So you will find that most people working many hours in angel investing either do this as a hobby or have combined their practice with a different business model. Of course, if you have been very successful in your career and have the luxury of retiring, you could eventually invest as an angel on a full-time basis, where you would not need a regular income but only look at the upside of those successful investments and take pleasure in helping startups take off.

How profitable is angel investing?

Angel investing offers many benefits for society and at a personal level. Most people still want to know how profitable it is. Several surveys have looked into this, including the ones done by Wharton University, Angel Capital Association, and Angel Resource Institute.

The findings show that in order to make money, one out of twenty companies needs to generate returns of 5x to 30x. Several companies that an angel invests in will remain 'zombie startups', companies that continue to exist but without an exit, such as a company sale, shares sale, or company wound up. The internal rate of return (IRR) for the angel portfolio of a pool of investors has shown around 22%, with an average old time of 4.5 years.

The same survey has found out that the more due diligence you do on the companies, the better the internal rate of return is, with a suggestion of spending at least 20 hours in companies that you end up investing in, in order to make your IRR positive. Another factor that helps increase the IRR is interacting frequently with the company post-investment, and a suggested frequency is once every other month.

At Angel Investor School, we have produced a simple spreadsheet that will allow you to see what the potential return of your angel investments are and how diversification will play an essential role in your returns.

The day to day of an angel

During our sessions at Angel Investor School, many active angel investors have shared with us what they do in their day-to-day lives. This allows us to picture what a day or a week in their lives might look like. One thing that is common is that they use email a lot (and more and more Whatsapp and other communication tools). Many have chosen to have some AI-enabled technology for their emails, such as Superhuman, as they can receive over 1000 (non-newsletter) emails in a week.

Active angels are exceptionally good at managing their time and have a pretty packed-up agenda.

Place yourself in the shoes of an average angel. In their life, they have got many roles. They are board members at a couple of companies they have founded; they are parents, and avid sportspersons.

They partition their day so that angel investing happens in the early morning and the evening after kids' bedtime.

While at work, they like attending meetings and speaking in conferences. They host private dinners for VCs and are often asked to speak in events as well as in the media. They take time to prepare their speeches and love to network during dinner, increasing their deal flow.

They may have an assistant who helps them look through all the pitch decks they receive and schedule meetings with the chosen few they want to learn more about.

They switch off in the afternoon and weekends for family time, as they enjoy seeing their family grow and playing with them.

They make themselves available for founders in their portfolio and share their phone number with them so that they know they can count on them when needed.

In the words of one of our distinguished ambassadors, Dan Scheinman:

I view my world as I want to spend about 50% of the time trying to find new companies. We'll probably talk about this in a bit. But in my world, there's basically only two strategies as an angel investor that makes sense. Focus and concentrate and choose a few things, or what they call spray and pray. Because you just don't know. Either strategy is somewhat rational saying,

I'm going to do a lot of deals, and I'm just gonna put a little amount of money into them. I've opted for the first strategy, I'm going to focus on a few things.

What I really like doing is going through decks and talking to the teams. 50% of my time has to be that at least, and trying to find that next one or two that I'm going to go do. Then, of course, doing diligence and making calls, trying to understand the market, calling my friends to get advice, and all that kind of stuff. Then the rest of the time really should be helping your existing portfolio of companies. In some cases I'm on the board, so it's board level, or in other cases, I'm just a friend of the founder, so I do it as a friend of the founder. I was early in a company called Treasure Data, which sold to Arm for a really good price.

The founder and I used to go to lunch with no agenda, once a month. Sometimes we will talk about his HR challenges. Sometimes we talk about the sales challenges, other times, we talked about when and where he should raise around and all that kind of stuff. But it was just a useful place for him to come to have a sounding board. I was not on the board, so he didn't have to worry about that situation. You could just talk freely about issues. It was a place I think that the founder felt safe and I certainly enjoyed doing it."

How often does an angel speak with the founders?

One question you might be asking yourself is, once you have invested in a company, how often should you be in touch with them. And what should you expect from the company?

These are questions that founders ask themselves too. When a founder expects too much contact, this is probably not a good sign, as this might mean they are a bit hesitant regarding where they should be steering the helm to. It could signal they can't run the company as they intended to or they need a lot of help (with contacts, how to scale, or with the business model itself). Too little contact is not good either, as the idea is to surround the company with people that can give a helping hand. In reality, it all depends on the conditions in which you are coming on board, and the support network that the startup already has in place.

Let's hear what Dan Scheinman has to say:

In early stage companies, generally you meet every six weeks and then in later stage companies, you meet once a quarter. So now all of a sudden, you have to prepare as a founder every six weeks to present where you are, and quite frankly, sometimes postage companies, things start going wrong or not enough has happened during the six week period. Sometimes you feel a little more pressure just from those meetings, and from the scheduling of those meetings than you do from before where it was very loose. Some founders I find, they're really a bit squirrelly.

They don't like that meeting that much early, because they find that preparing for it, and then having it, that it kind of impedes them and impedes their ability to be freewheeling. Some founders resist quite frankly, or have meaningless board meetings just to check the box. I think the good founders try and get something out of it. In fact, there's one founder who we were on the board and continually does it, they will say, look, my number one problem is this. And that's what we're going to talk about that we're not going to worry about all the plethora of other issues and numbers and blah, blah, blah, here's the number one problem I have. Maybe it's that the customers are taking too long to decide or we built a set of features that turned out that the market didn't want. Now I got to figure out, do I keep doubling down on those or do I do something else? Whatever it is. Then they will just turn those six week meaning into kind of a focus on that, get people's opinion, and then go back and fix it. That to me, is one of the more effective formats for an early stage company."

Many times you will join an investment in the form of a secondary angel or through a syndicate. This is a type of 'passive' angel investing, and if you are lucky, you will receive regular reports on how the startup is doing. You will probably just sit back and relax and hope for the best. Your best contribution might be to follow-on investments when these are needed, or attracting other fellow angels or VCs when more funding is required (as it inevitably will).

However, if you happen to be a lead angel investor or a strategic investor, you might be involved a lot more. As an angel, you can become a mentor to the company, a paid advisor, and even take a seat on the board of directors. Moreover, many times founders rely on angel investors for their network of contacts that may take the startup to the next level or even open the door for a sales contract or government approval.

Whatever your role is as an angel investor, you need to know yourself inside out and figure out what your value-added can be and how you can set these expectations truthfully, as this will attract deals your way.

Setting expectations

What is really important is that, as an angel investor, you set up expectations clearly. Before you sign the term sheet and wire the funds across, think to yourself what you are willing to give to the company in terms of your commitment. What are you aiming to gain from this investment? If you are just looking for a return on your money, you might take a laid-back approach. If you are looking for training in a field or specific area, you might want to keep closer to the company.

It is good to be transparent with the founders, not only with what you are giving but why you are giving, so that they are not surprised when you start asking for detailed updates. By having radical honesty, we find that things turn up working better.

Once you have begun a relationship, take your time to review whether your expectations are being met and whether you are meeting the expectations of the other parties. This works both when things are going well and when things are not going so great.

Our ambassador Gokul Rajaram adds his knowledge:

The earlier the company, the more help they need, and the more frequently, the angel should keep checking in with the company. So the company is essentially pre-product, and it's simply a team of folks. Many times what happens is the CEO, there's a team of engineers working on the product, and the CEO is trying to figure out the right way to go to market. At that point, you need to essentially be there for them. So the way I think of it as many CEOs, many founders try to say, let's set up a regularly scheduled meeting.

But I think instead of a regularly scheduled meeting, what is more helpful is to be there on demand. At startups things happen without any warning. So if you want if you schedule a meeting for Monday, it's not just on Monday that something's going to happen. It could happen on Tuesday. So instead, what I do is I give my cell phone number to every founder, and they know that they can text me at any point, whenever something essentially happens in the company that they need input, help, advice, feedback. And within two hours or three hours, we'll find the time to quickly do a Zoom, or get on the phone and chat.

With some founders we have almost a back and forth text message stream going on even outside of the times we talk. Then other founders don't actually take me up and might message me once every three to six months. Sometimes not even that, sometimes it is good to know of it when there is the next financing round. I think ultimately you are a service. You can't force something on the founder, the founder has to pull. I firmly believe that the angel investor should not push. Ultimately, you're here to serve the founders. It is the same as a board member. One of the lessons I've learned is a board is not there to push and prescribe. Ultimately, it's the founder and team that are running the company. You need to always remind them that you're here, you need to remind them what your capabilities are, what value you can add. But ultimately, they have to pull you; they have to be the ones taking initiative."

Let's have a look at some roles you may be performing, starting with the strategic investor role.

Being a strategic investor

The best startups take in investors not because they need their money but because they realize that the angel can become an asset for their growth and scaling. This is the type of investor that you want to be known as, and if you crack the list of qualities and assets that you can provide a company, then you are on your way to becoming more desirable and having people begging you to come on board. Think of how many people would like to get Bill Gates or Elon Musk as an angel investor in their companies. And you can become the king of your particular niche. For example, Fabrice Grinda is a name well known to founders building platforms and marketplaces. When they research investors that have contributed to successful platforms, they seem to find that his early-stage investments make a difference and allow startups to make it to Series A and beyond. Moreover, Dan Martell has grown to be one of the best investors and coaches in SaaS companies, and having his name as investor is a great presentation card for VCs down the line.

The more companies you invest in and offer your help, the stronger your knowledge will be and more popular you will become in the startup community.

When an angel offers a specific strength that they have that is relevant to a company, this can become more valuable than funds, and it could even be worth giving some extra equity/options to this person. Strengths can come either in process knowledge, industry knowledge, and network knowledge.

So, in short, when you meet with founders, be clear on what you will be contributing and how often you will be doing so. Do also have in mind that the fact that you are giving them money does not necessarily mean you can demand anything from the founders. Capital is abundant, so if startups are desperate for money and won't take your skills and network into consideration, it may be a red flag when writing that check.

Being a mentor

Angel investors have gained a bigger role as mentors of startups. Without the biggest vested interest in the company, they can become a great sounding board for founders that want to share ideas and learn in a safe environment, without sounding challenging or silly in front of co-founders or the company board. This is especially true when the angel has got a background in entrepreneurship and has fought similar battles to the ones that the startup is currently facing. This could be in the business area, but also the work-life balance area.

Passionate angels can be really helpful to founders and take huge pleasure in helping them out. This may be one of the biggest rewards for angels. For a mentor, feeling instrumental in the growth of a company is a big enough reward in exchange for their efforts. It makes them feel valued, especially for the ones that have already retired from the day-to-day action.

For a company, showing they are involved with mentorship adds credibility. Having credible and successful people associated with the company can help the startup grow.

A company can have more than one mentor, as different people can fulfill different roles. Some of them will be more industry-focused, providing expert insights into the industry that the startup is tackling. Others will be growth-focused, having won many battles growing small businesses and sharing their growth hacking techniques. Finally, others are more people-focused, and they can help relieve the pressure that a startup founder experiences while dealing with their anxieties and worries.

If you are starting a mentorship, it is best to keep it informal and fluid at first. This allows people to measure the chemistry in the relationship and the level of engagement. If the relationship becomes more frequent and adds value, it might be useful to formalize it. This may mean capturing things on paper, such as actions to be taken, and it might also imply having compensation for the time that the mentor is dedicating.

Being a coach

Many people take coaching and mentoring as synonyms, when in fact, they are not the same. Mentoring is more of a long-term, informal approach to learning from somebody that is more experienced.

Coaching, on the other hand, is used by people to improve in the short term. The coach doesn't necessarily need to know the specific skills that sit in the domain of the coachee. People that practice coaching have studied and sometimes certified their coaching learning, are good at asking questions, following up, and prompting people to take uncomfortable actions that will make a difference.

One of our ambassadors, Dan Martell, uses several hats, but one of the main ones is his coaching one. He has created a methodology and a company around his name that delivers top coaching for SaaS founders. In Dan's own words:

I've been doing this (angel investing) for 14 years. Today, I'm not actively involved in my investments the way I had been in the past. The reason why is I just don't have the time. I coach, literally the best founders, they invest in their coaching at a very significant level. I'm one of the top coaches in the world. So I wouldn't feel comfortable coaching a founder, and then giving the same level of time and attention to an investment portfolio that didn't pay me.

Three years ago, it just didn't make sense to me anymore. So now I tell people that when I invest, my money is my capital, you can use my name, which has value to open up doors. And every once in a while, you can reach out if you need introductions. But no, I'm not here as your coach, because that is the aspect of my life that people invest in. If you want to talk about that we can, but honestly, for a lot of the early stage people, it's just too early for my private coaching. In the past 100%. It's where I learned how to not only, because there's one thing a lot of coaches are, may have had success themselves, although honestly, most have not. It's kind of, you know, teachers or people that couldn't make it like, there's a bunch of sayings around that, like coaches or people that can't actually build companies themselves. I've always been an operator.

I did reverse engineering, how I teach people. What I'm most proud of is getting results for SaaS founders, consistently. In short, I'm an investor, not a coach when I give my money, but my personal network in my association definitely creates a lot of value for the entrepreneurs where it makes sense."

Becoming part of an advisory board

In an advisory board, typically, an experienced professional is asked for advice and direction; they will be mentioned in pitch decks and asked to perform a series of tasks such as recruiting and business development. Their name will be used in pitch decks to show there are important people that trust this company and are inputting their time and valuable lessons into it. It also shows that the founders have been able to convince some heavyweights into participating in the development of the startup.

However, there might be a conflict of interest for the advisor. Let's hear what Dan Scheinman has to say about this:

For me, as a professional investor, if you were to call me and say I'm founding a technology company, and I'd be great to have you as an advisor. For me, what that means, because I have some number of shares, I inherit a conflict of interest where I can't do anything competitively. And I'm not getting enough shares to make it that interesting and I don't have my own capital at work. So for me, it's a non-value-add proposition. For some folks who like to have a lot of investments and who are not all that involved, they view it as a positive thing because they say, well, just another one, it's free equity, I'll do whatever

the founder needs, and I'll do it. Let's say you might get a 10th of a percent, maybe a little more but somewhere in there as an advisor, then after it dilutes, you're not getting very much. You're lending your brand and then saying, I'm not going to do anything in conflict. And so that becomes the challenge."

Taking a seat as an advisor (and/or in the board of directors) may also raise your profile as an angel if the companies take off, so it is something worth considering if you believe in the founders and the team you are investing in.

Taking a seat on the board of directors

A board of directors is something that evolves with time as a company grows bigger. When the company is just a two-man band, it doesn't make a lot of sense to have a board of directors, as the team members will be meeting frequently together. However, at later stages, a more formal arrangement is necessary. When you invest as an angel with significant influence, you might be offered, or you may require a seat in the board of directors. This is something that normally VCs request (depending on the company's size, the investment, and the stage), but boards can easily include angel investors.

Let's hear what our ambassador Anthony Thomson has got to say about the role of a director inside a board:

You have to separate out the two roles there because investors are the owners of the business. The managers are the people who look after it on a day to day basis for them. The investors entrust to the management their money and rely upon the business, the entrepreneurs, the people in the business to

deliver the business plan that they presented to the investor. So, that's the first role of an investor, to be the owner of that part of the business. The management has a responsibility to those people. Then if you want to sit on the advisory board or on the board of the business itself; you have two roles. You have your role as a shareholder, and then you have a role as someone whose role is to help build the business for you, but also for all of the other channels for all of the other others. I would always counsel any entrepreneur never to forget who owns the business. It is the shareholders."

If you join one board, it is great that you can bring perspective to the team, that you can question and push back on their actions and ideas, that you can be proactive with new ideas on what a company can do to tackle their problems, and that you can provide strategic thought. Another area where value can be added is by offering governance and oversight, and this is one thing that directors are obliged to do by law.

When looking at things to be avoided, a board member should try to avoid showing up to meetings unprepared, taking up a lot of time in meetings, and attacking the team or the CEO destructively.

When helping, one of the key priorities of directors should be recruiting. This may come in the form of suggesting great people that should join the company and also interviewing potential candidates. Supporting fundraising is another great help for companies, as CEOs are generally very time-constrained by this activity. Risk management is another key task for board members, and setting up proper controls and keeping on top of the company's accounts is really important. Good governance and risk management will be fundamental when fundraising, as it will be easier for VCs and investors to write checks to sound companies that have strong oversight.

As a part of this same topic, evaluating the firm's CEO is of utmost importance, as the boat captain may at times need help to develop certain skills or may even need replacing. Finally, because directors have got a fiduciary responsibility toward shareholders, to maximize the value of the firm, the directors should look at the exit strategy of the firm and ensure it is always up to date.

Let's hear what Dan Scheinman has to say about it:

My personal view has been, I never demand a board seat. When I come in, I'm generally one to two and a half percent of the company somewhere in there in that early round, and then I get diluted down over time. My actual goal, quite frankly, Zoom ended up with about 1.2% at the IPO, I want to end up about 1%. Because my thesis is if I had a fund, I get 5%. then let's say 20% carry, it would be 1%. But what I do is I basically say to founders, if you want me to be on the board, let me know and that's something I might do. But I'm not going to push you on this, this is up to you. I've had the privilege of being selected onto the board of Arista Networks, which is a $15 billion public company, and Zoom, which is like a $60 billion public company.

All by the founders, they asked me to join the board and help them and I've been privileged to go do so. I'm on three startup boards right now. The primary role of the board of directors early is actually to make sure that the entrepreneur is on track for the next round. This is a marathon with 18 months sprints. The reality is what you're doing is you're sprinting from one funding round to the next funding round. What we want to do is make sure that the company is capitalised and is hitting its milestones so that it can get passed to the next set of investors.

And so really what we spend time doing is trying to talk strategy with the entrepreneur. Although we never do it in this way, it's basically resource allocation. What you find is some founders are really a product first. So what happens is 95% of the resource will end up in engineering and 5% in sales, which may lead to challenges. It's the job of the board to say, wait a second, we can't be allocating, 95% to the product side, we've got to be more balanced, right. Or we have some founders who are completely sales and they are under resource engineering. The key I think of good boards early is to help the founders with introductions, help keep the founders focused on the goals and the milestones. If possible, even help them to avoid things which require more capital before the next round, because the most diluted rounds of the founders and to the early investors are these bridge rounds. The more you can avoid them, and be capital efficient, the better it is for all the early investors and employees."

Some top angel investors you should know about

It is common to see successful entrepreneurs become angel investors, as well as venture capitalists, and we thought you should know of some of the best-known investors, as these can act as great role models.

You probably have heard of Ron Conway, a Silicon Valley-based investor, who invested early in Paypal and Google. He ran Angel Investors LP for a few years and created SV Angels. He has been an active angel investor since the mid-90s and has received wide recognition for his role in the tech ecosystem. He has won several awards: he was included on Vanity Fair's 100 most influential people in the Information Age in 2010, awarded Best Angel at the 2009 TechCrunch Crunchies Awards, and has been named on Forbes Magazine Midas list of top "deal-makers" since 2011. Certainly, one of the biggest names still around.

Another name that may ring a bell is Dave McClure, the founder of 500 startups. He is the founder of Practical Venture Capital and has been an investor and entrepreneur in Silicon Valley for over twenty-five years. Previously he was the founding partner of 500 Startups, a global VC firm and startup accelerator with over $500M in assets under management. Dave has invested in hundreds of companies around the world, including more than 15 unicorns and 5 IPOs. His investments include Sendgrid, Twilio, Lyft, Slideshare, Mint.com and Lucid. He was named by Forbes as one of the top VCs in the world in 2016 and 2017 (Forbes Midas List)

Another investor you should know about is Marc Andreessen, an entrepreneur, investor, and coding guru. He developed Mosaic, the first internet browser, which later sold to AOL for $4.2 billion. He also co-founded Loudcloud, which as Opsware, sold to Hewlett-Packard for $1.6 billion. Andreessen created Andreessen's venture capital firm Andreessen Horowitz, ranked the number one venture capital firm on several occasions.

A big champion of angel investing, Naval Ravikant is an Indian-American entrepreneur and investor. He co-founded AngelList. He has invested early-stage in over 200 companies, including Uber, FourSquare, Twitter, Wish.com, Poshmark, Postmates, Thumbtack, Notion, SnapLogic, Opendoor, Clubhouse, Stack Overflow, OpenDNS, Yammer, and Clearview AI, with over 70 total exits and more than 10 Unicorn companies. He is, without a doubt, one of the most innovative minds in venture capital. He created incredibly valuable resources like VentureHacks & AngelList for entrepreneurs and angel investors.

Finally, Mark Cuban is another hot name in the community. He has been an entrepreneur since childhood. Extremely smart, well-connected, and passionate, Mark started selling garbage bags door to door. After a dispute with an employer who wanted him to clean instead of closing an important sale, Mark created MicroSolutions, a computer consulting service. He went on to later sell MicroSolutions in 1990 to CompuServe. In 1995, Mark and long-time friend Todd Wagner came up with an internet-based solution to not being able to listen to Hoosiers Basketball games out in Texas. That solution was Broadcast.com – streaming audio over the internet. In just four short years, Broadcast.com would be sold to Yahoo for $5.6 billion dollars. Mark is chairman and CEO of AXS TV, one of ABC's "Sharks" on the hit show Shark Tank, and an investor in an ever-growing business portfolio.

The way to being a super angel: the story of Fabrice Grinda

Several angels have decided to create their own venture capital firm focusing on early-stage firms. This is the example of the super angel Fabrice Grinda, who decided to open up FJ Labs together with his partner and friend Jose Marin. Fabrice had always liked being an entrepreneur, but also helping other founders, so investing in their firms was a good complement to his time invested in listening to others.

Fabrice started his angel career with seven investments within two years, and he was lucky enough to have successful exits on six of them. He then had a chance to invest in a more aggressive way when his startup OLX grew, and his cash flow improved. He developed a strategy to filter companies within one hour. Fabrice rejects most companies he sees, but provides very useful feedback on what doesn't fit with his investment thesis and provide direction.

While making 10-25 investments per year, he realized a lot of administrative work had to be done and decided to get his assistant to sign all paperwork without carefully reading it. This is not a recommended strategy for any investor, though it worked well for him at the time. After a few years, he partnered with Jose Marin, the co-founder of DeRemate.com, to co-invest in deals. It was a good partnership, as Jose was more meticulous with paperwork and legals.

After exiting OLX, Fabrice continued investing in startups and looked for external capital. He found Telenor, an international telco provider as an investor who valued Fabrice's foresight into the future of the economy and platforms. They got $50 million in investment, and from that point, the company continued growing stronger. They currently employ more than 30 people that have been divided into several tasks so that Fabrice and Jose can focus on meeting the founders and sussing them out.

Successful angel, successful VC? The story of Ullas Naik

Fabrice's story is not the only one when turning into institutional investment. It is also interesting to look at the story of Ullas Naik, another Angel Investor School ambassador. He shows how some people go for personal angel investing first, to learn the ropes, before embarking on a venture capitalist journey.

His first investment was in 1995 as an angel, and then he made 12 investments within three years. Six of them became multibillion-dollar companies. He realized that in that process of evaluating and choosing startups, he would have a lot more fun than stock picking in Wall Street. This, in turn, became his first glance at venture capital. In 1999, he was pretty burnt out with Wall Street and thought he was ready to jump in full into venture capitalism as a career.

When moving, he acknowledged that with angel investing, he could certainly take a lot more risk. For example, choosing companies that perhaps might not be investable as an institutional investor, for example, when performing due diligence wasn't possible. When moving into an institutional investor role, he recognized that the premise is to stick to an investment thesis and a point of view on a market opportunity.

Angel investing allowed Ullas to jump into fast-moving situations without doing exhaustive due diligence. When he designed Streamlined Ventures, he aimed to keep it very flexible, a bit similar to how an angel behaves. He introduced a model where he is the only GP in the fund.

In his view, the amount of work required as an institutional investor is much higher, with hundreds of hours researching the companies and entrepreneurs in order to comply with fiduciary duties to LPs and also to increase the odds of success in those companies.

The story of Eneko Knörr and AngelClub.es

One of our distinguished ambassadors, Eneko Knörr, has got a lot of experience in setting up a club. He is a Spanish serial entrepreneur and investor with experience of more than 20 years in tech startups. He was named business angel of the Year by the Spanish Business Angel Networks Association in 2018 and best investor by the New York summit in 2015, honorific professor at the University of Vasque Country, and an associate professor at IE Business School in Madrid.

After several successful investments, he was asked by many starting angels that they would like to invest in the deals that he was investing in; he decided to open up AngelClub.es, which began with a very low-tech model, a periodic email newsletter. AngelClub is free to join, and it gives people the opportunity to co-invest with him, mostly in regional deals. He takes a commission for the investment made for the management of the investment. He invests globally but mostly in Spanish startups, where his strengths lie. Eneko believes every angel should start their journey co-investing with more experienced people. In his own words:

If you are an outsider and you get started and you don't know anyone, you're not gonna get the good deals. So you're gonna get the deals that have probably been rejected by other investors. So networking is super important and getting to know all the entrepreneurs and all the investors and getting inside this small network is super important. I think it could be very convenient for someone that is starting to try to get into one of these syndicates or these angel clubs to try to get the best deals."

Enter the Angels' Den of Bill Morrow

Another of our ambassadors, Bill Morrow, has founded a company called Angels Den, one of the largest investor clubs. At the time of writing, it had an international presence in over ten countries. Angels Den Funding carefully matches start-ups with a suitable lead investor before opening the funding to a wider investor network. The lead investor typically has sector expertise and is willing to conduct due diligence and provide mentorship to help the business grow.

Through Angels Den, Bill curates deals, teaches angels, matches lead investors with startups, and carefully scrutinizes investments. He came up with the idea after watching TV shows like Dragons' Den and Shark Tank. He looked at the questions that people were asking there and tried to prepare the founders of businesses to express theirs in a way that even TV people could understand. He was trying to do something good for the marketplace and set up in 2007. By that time, many people were looking to invest and disillusioned with the solutions in the marketplace. Years later, there's 22,000 investors looking across the world interested in investing through his club. Angels' Den prides itself on more than ten years in equity investment, organizing around 50 events a year and having a record of 92% of funded deals still in business.

When to quit

Nobody says that angel investing is a lifelong career, though many decide to run it for many years after they retire.

You need to ask yourself regularly whether you are getting what you wanted out of the experience. This may be financial rewards, learning possibilities, exposure to new ideas and startups, networking, and influence.

All in all, the experience needs to be rewarding, and it should not produce too much stress and affect your work / life balance. We recommend an annual review of your strategy and set some KPIs that will tell you whether this occupation is doing what it needs to do in the long run.

Rounding it up

Congratulations for reading this far! If you have managed to make it all the way here, chances are you are interested in becoming an angel investor. You will contribute value to the world, and in return, you'll hopefully have the time of your life. You may have already made your first investment and could be heading towards that dreamt home run that will produce a new unicorn, change people's lives and make a killing in terms of returns.

If you are still on the fences, remember that life is always unexpected, and you never know what you will get. They say the only constant thing in life is change, so embrace it. And those that don't take any chances don't get very far. Remember to surround yourself with successful and interesting people, as chances are you end up being as rich and as happy as the average of the people that you meet with.

If you believe you would like intensive training on how to become and conduct yourself as a successful angel investor, you can always join us at Angel Investor School. We teach different programs on angel investing, and we bring together the top angels in the world. We await you with open arms.

www.ingramcontent.com/pod-product-compliance
Lightning Source LLC
Chambersburg PA
CBHW060825220526
45466CB00003B/984